Jesus, Judaism, and Christian Anti-Judaism

Jesus, Judaism, and Christian Anti-Judaism

Reading the New Testament after the Holocaust

PAULA FREDRIKSEN

AND

ADELE REINHARTZ

EDITORS

Westminster John Knox Press
LOUISVILLE • LONDON

Scripture quotations, unless otherwise indicated, are from the New Revised Standard Version of the Bible, copyright © 1989 by the Division of Christian Education of the National Council of the Churches of Christ in the U.S.A., and are used by permission.

Book design by Sharon Adams
Cover design by Jennifer K. Cox

First edition
Published by Westminster John Knox Press
Louisville, Kentucky

This book is printed on acid-free paper that meets the American National Standards Institute Z39.48 standard. ∞

PRINTED IN THE UNITED STATES OF AMERICA

02 03 04 05 06 07 08 09 10 11 — 10 9 8 7 6 5 4 3 2 1

Library of Congress Cataloging-in-Publication Data

Jesus, Judaism, and Christian anti-Judaism : reading the New Testament after the Holocaust / Paula Fredriksen and Adele Reinhartz, editors.
    p. cm.
    Includes bibliographical references.
    ISBN 0-664-22328-1 (pbk.)
    1. Bible. N.T.—Criticism, interpretation, etc. 2. Jesus Christ. 3. Jews in the New Testament. I. Fredriksen, Paula, 1951–. II. Reinhartz, Adele, 1953–

    BS2370 .J47 2002
    261.2'6'09015

                                   2002071319

To Krister Stendahl

Pastor and Scholar

Tireless Worker in the Vineyard of Jewish-Christian Relations

Contents

Foreword

The main point of Tom Friedman's fascinating and often provocative book *The Lexus and the Olive Tree* rests entirely on the two images that dominate its title. The images effectively rivet the reader's attention on the way in which global economic growth (the Lexus) is a clear and present danger to particular cultural identity (the Olive Tree). Like a second Flood of biblical proportion, the global democratization of technology, finance, and information threatens to efface all that stands in its way.

While Friedman, admittedly, does not directly take up contemporary Christian-Jewish interfaith dialogue, what he chronicles in his award-winning book does, indirectly, speak to the issue. Christians and Jews, synagogues and churches, face a common set of challenges. Specifically, how is it, amidst the homogenizing and totalizing power of economic globalization, that particular faith communities—like those of Judaism and Christianity—will be able to preserve, let alone deepen, their specific religious heritage? If our world's post–Cold War economy has proven itself no respecter of culture, neither will it be a respecter of religion. The implication of Friedman's analysis is clear: Jews and Christians are in the same boat. Both will struggle mightily to preserve their own respective traditions.

But if Christians and Jews are to find, and even make, common cause in the post–Cold War era, then it is a pre–Cold War event that still requires attention. The systematic extermination of European Jews during the middle of the last century still casts a long, dark shadow over our world. That shadow also lingers over modern Jewish-Christian relations.

Contemporary Jews have worked hard to find meaning in this horror, preserving its memory and wrestling with its lessons, in the firm commitment that something like this will never happen again, to Jews or to anyone else. But Christian churches have only begun to understand how to embrace and express their unique missionary enterprise in light of the Holocaust. Particularly, Christianity has not yet come to grips with its own complicity in the Holocaust. While no one will argue that contemporary Christians were actively engaged in and thus responsible for this mass murder, it is unarguably the case that Christianity developed and fostered—often implicitly, sometimes explicitly—a principled anti-Judaism. And Christian anti-Judaism did, in fact, contribute directly to the Holocaust.

Moreover, and to the point of this book: An examination of the sources of Christian anti-Judaism drives us back to the New Testament and to the history of its interpretation. It is one thing for Christians to claim that a new revelation (the New Testament) presents the key to the interpretation of an existing set of sacred texts (the Old Testament). But it is another matter altogether when this new set of texts either communicates or encourages Christian anti-Judaism. The potentially anti-Jewish character of the New Testament is therefore a crucial issue in contemporary Jewish-Christian dialogue.

We are thus in a serious dilemma. Both Christians and Jews face the common challenges of maintaining particular and historically connected faiths in the face of an impending deluge of economic globalization. However, for Christians and Jews to find common cause, they must build mutual understanding, one that assesses the way in which the New Testament itself (and/or a particular set of interpretations) may foster Christian anti-Judaism. This is the project of *Jesus, Judaism, and Christian Anti-Judaism*. The present book is compelling and needed, simply because it honestly and directly addresses this difficult subject. Mutual understanding and common cause can be achieved only by frank discussion about what stands between us.

But this book also tantalizes with all sorts of possibilities. For example, some Christian readers will be intrigued to discover that ancient Judaism was not a religion of "works righteousness"; that "Judaism" was not the "opponent" of either Jesus or Paul; that, in fact, both Jesus and Paul were good Jews; that neither the first Gospels, nor Jesus himself, are likely to have been sources of Christian anti-Judaism; that, in its earliest incarnations, Christianity was just another way of being Jewish; and that many of Christianity's anti-Jewish assumptions originated in a line of interpretation stemming from the Christian Reformation (and not from the New Testament itself). However, it may well disturb some of us to learn the Gospel of John probably does encourage a strongly anti-Jewish perspective, as does the early Christian interpretation of the New Testament.

So, who should read a book like this, one that excites its readers with new historical information and perspective at the same time as it openly and truthfully addresses difficult and painful questions? Having taught in faith-related colleges and theological seminaries, I can easily see this book being used as a text by students preparing for service in either a synagogue or a church. But, as an ordained minister and as someone who has served the Christian church for all of his adult life, I see yet another audience. This book should be read by Jewish and Christian laypersons alike, simply because it candidly tackles a crucial aspect of meaningful and lasting dialogue between the communities of our two great faiths. How should the book be used? I will be so bold as to suggest several possible uses. It would serve well as a basic textbook for college, university, and seminary courses in early Christianity, in Jewish-Christian dialogue, and in the history of anti-Semitism. In addition, it could well form the basis of interfaith study groups, from both synagogues and churches, who agree to meet for several weeks to read and discuss the chapters. In advocating this, I join with the authors who deeply desire that a lasting peace, shalom, be established between Jews and Christians.

Carey C. Newman
Passover / Easter 2002
Baylor University

Introduction

Paula Fredriksen and Adele Reinhartz

Both of the editors of this book teach at universities about ancient Jews and Christians, and about ancient Judaism and Christianity. The subjects we treat, the historical evidence we survey, and the methods of analysis that we try to teach to our students often make for very dense lectures: this material is not the stuff of sermons. To share the excitement and the insights that can come from the historical investigation of Jesus or Paul with people in the pew—be those pews in churches or in synagogues—we frequently lecture in various faith communities and at interfaith gatherings. The passionate engagement of our many audiences with these challenging historical materials has consistently confirmed our own sense of the larger importance of our work. We know, from personal experience, that the academic study of ancient Christianity matters to people outside the academy too.

That conviction accounts for this book. Its goal, quite simply, is to make available to nonacademic readers some of the best current scholarship in the study of ancient Christianity. The colleagues whom we invited into this project are all active and internationally recognized authorities on the New Testament, late Second Temple Judaism, and early Christianity. E. P. Sanders of Duke University has written books of fundamental importance on Paul, on Jesus, and on ancient Jewish practice and belief. John Gager of Princeton University has several books placing ancient Christian movements within their various social contexts; he has most recently written specifically on Paul. A.-J. Levine of Vanderbilt University has done pioneering work on the Gospel of Matthew, its sources, and the roles of Jews, Gentiles, men, and women in Matthew's community. Paula Fredriksen and Adele Reinhartz have each published several books on the earliest Christian communities, on Jesus, and on the various representations of Jesus in the Gospels.

1

More than common intellectual interests and mutual respect brought us together for this volume, however. Each of us, in our respective writings, has continually explored, challenged, and addressed the issue of anti-Judaism in the New Testament and in New Testament interpretation. We are each acutely aware of the morally and historically distorting effect that Christian anti-Judaism has had within scholarship in our own fields of research and—in terrible ways, within living memory—within our larger culture.

Anti-Jewish traditions run deep in church teachings in large part because they rest on particular readings of Christianity's core canon, namely, the four Gospels and the Letters of Paul. Throughout the long centuries that stand between the earliest followers of Jesus and ourselves, these readings have come to have the force and weight of historical description: what these particular traditions teach has come to be seen as what Jesus and Paul themselves taught. Unless we can distinguish between Paul and his interpreters, gauge the distance that separates Jesus' words and acts from the Gospels' renditions of his teachings, or measure the gap between the Gospels and their subsequent interpretations, we have little hope of overcoming Christian anti-Judaism.

Anti-Jewish traditions, whether they are present in the New Testament or in the subsequent history of interpretation, arose within particular historical contexts. Few Christians can know about these contexts, however, unless they enroll in academic courses on Christian origins, or do extensive scholarly reading on their own, or have a priest, preacher, or community leader who does and who shares. But academic writing can be obscure, intimidating, or just plain opaque (to academics as well as to lay readers!). Popular writing, which frequently draws uncritically on familiar (usually noncritical) interpretive understandings, is more often part of the problem than part of the solution.

We put together this book, *Jesus, Judaism, and Christian Anti-Judaism*, with exactly these concerns in mind. We and our colleagues have endeavored to write as simply, lucidly, and clearly as possible. We have organized our essays around the historical figures and canonical texts that matter the most to Christian communities, and whose interpretation has contributed to Christianity's often hostile characterizations of Jews and Judaism. A select annotated bibliography gives suggestions for further reading. We hope that this collection of essays will prove interesting and useful to many different kinds of readers and for a variety of contexts, including university, college, and seminary courses in New Testament as well as for adult Bible study groups.

Paula Frediksen's essay opens the collection with an overview of the birth and development of Christianity within the cradle of broader Mediterranean culture. Her time frame stretches from the early first century, with the mission of Jesus, into the fourth century and beyond, with the conversion of Christianity under Constantine. As the identity (and, linked immediately to identity, the theology) of certain types of Gentile Christianities develop, beginning in the second century, she explains, so too grows the construction and use of demeaning views of Judaism to express that theology. These did double duty, providing a way to argue with other Christians about how to read the Bible, as well as a way to define oneself and one's own group. "Jews" as a theological abstraction became *the* Christian antitype. This way of thinking about Jews dominated the orthodox interpretation of Scriptures, both Old Testament and New. This theme then determined the church's view of its own origins, conceived as having developed, beginning from Jesus' own mission, in contrast and even in opposition to Judaism.

E. P. Sanders, in chapter 2, describes and explains the modern quest of the historical Jesus while also presenting his own portrait of this elusive ancient figure. Along the way, Sanders explains many salient features of Jesus' native religious context, late Second Temple Judaism. Acts of piety and attitudes toward holiness that moderns often find mystifying or even offensive in ancient religion, such as blood sacrifices or concepts of purity, receive particular attention. In explaining these points, Sanders draws attention to the frequent evidence in the Gospels and in Paul's letters for Jesus' and his apostles' full participation in Jewish cult: it was a normal and natural feature of their religious landscape. The reader will come away with a fresh sense of Jesus' own piety, with an appreciation for what constitutes modern Christian anti-Judaism in both its scholarly and its popular manifestations, and, finally, with ways to distinguish such anti-Judaism from simply bad—that is, anachronistic or historically uninformed—readings of the Gospels.

John Gager next brings the reader to the historical Paul. To do so, he removes the layers of traditionally anti-Jewish readings of Paul even as he explains how these came to exist. Reconstructing Paul's life as a Pharisee before he joined the new movement, Gager offers an explanation for Paul's missionary focus on Gentiles while explaining that such a focus was itself native to Paul's own religious culture, namely, Diaspora Judaism. Gager concludes his presentation with biblical exegesis. He lifts up verses from Paul's letters that have been traditionally viewed as expressing Paul's repudiation of Judaism, and shows how, understood within the historical context that he has reconstructed, they mean no such thing.

Amy-Jill Levine considers the Synoptic Gospels, their historical contexts, and the communities in which and for which they were written. She explains that historical-critical analysis, that is, an approach to ancient texts that takes their historical contexts fully into account, cannot definitively say whether a text was intended to inspire scorn or hatred for Jews who did not believe Jesus to be the messiah. Nevertheless, she urges, one can propose plausible, and compelling, alternative interpretations of texts that have traditionally been read as anti-Jewish. She concludes that it is essential to expose both the traditionally anti-Jewish readings as well as those passages that lend themselves to such readings. Such material should not be glossed over or simply proclaimed problem-free. Settings in which Jews and Christians study these texts together may be the best forum in which to undertake this sometimes painful, always important, task.

Adele Reinhartz examines the ways that Jews and Judaism appear in the Gospel of John. She argues that John weaves together three interrelated stories: a narrative about the historical Jesus, a story about the Johannine community for which this Gospel was a central document, and a story about the universe that also tells about God's relationship to humankind. She concludes that anti-Judaism is deeply embedded within all these narrative strands, each of which assigns Jews to the negative poles (darkness versus light, error versus truth) that structure its message and story. An awareness of the historical, social, and religious contexts in which the Gospel was written does not undo its anti-Judaism. But understanding the specific circumstances that shaped this Gospel enables the reader to see that these ancient, negative attitudes need not and should not be normative for Christian communities today.

Five scholars, five opinions. We are all independent researchers. Despite our unanimity on the importance of understanding history for interpreting early Christianity, and our broad agreement on many issues, we have our differences, too. No effort has been made to smooth these over or to disguise them. Each essay presents a point of view and provides evidence and arguments in support of that view; in the next essay, a contrary opinion, again with evidence and argument, might well appear. This is all part of the rough-and-tumble of active research, and the measure, too, of how difficult it can be to achieve a clear view of the past. We do not all agree on whether and when it is appropriate to refer to the earliest followers of Jesus as "Christians." Nor do we agree on specific historical issues such as the presence of missionary activity among first-century Jews. John Gager holds that Paul had long been involved in a mission to Gentiles, not only after his call to join the Jesus movement, but also before (p. 65). Paula Fredriksen argues that Jews received converts, but disputes that they actively solicited them (p. 15): an actual *mission* to Gentiles, demanding that they abandon their ancestral gods and make a unique commitment to the God of Israel first appears, she thinks, only with the Christian mission itself. Finally, we do not all agree on whether anti-Judaism is present primarily in the history of the Christian interpretation of the New Testament or whether it is also present in the New Testament writings themselves. John Gager and Paula Fredriksen place much of the onus on the ancient history of interpretation; E. P. Sanders places much emphasis on the modern, supposedly academic, one as well. Amy-Jill Levine and Adele Reinhartz do not exclude the strong possibility that the Gospels themselves share some of the responsibility. In retaining these differences, and in agreeing to disagree, we invite our readers to appreciate the complexity of these issues, and we call on them to read, learn, and participate in the discussion with us.

Our hope is that this volume will contribute in positive ways to the efforts of lay readers to understand the historical circumstances of early Christianity. By making this effort, such readers will be able to see how anti-Judaism entered Christian theology at a formative stage of its development, defining the church's mentality (grace *as opposed to* law; works *as opposed to* faith, prayer *as opposed to* sacrifice) while determining the church's interpretation of foundational New Testament texts. We also hope that this book will help readers to see that we have other interpretive possibilities and available readings when, with historical understanding, we approach Christian Scriptures. Readings that neither distort history nor encourage prejudice. Readings that enhance Christian self-understanding. Readings that can promote peace.

As historians, we work in a nontheological key. Each of us, in the larger body of our various works and in the particular essays that we present here, seeks in different ways to close the gap between Judaism and Christianity as they are imagined to have been in the first century. We argue, and by the presentation of historical data we seek to demonstrate, that first-century Judaism was first-century Christianity's context and its content, not its contrast; that this Judaism was not Christianity's background, but its matrix. Think otherwise, and it becomes impossible to understand, much less to see, the two historical figures who stand as the churches' foundation, namely, Jesus and Paul. Think otherwise, and it becomes impossible to hear what they said.

As scholars of ancient Christianity who are also committed to interfaith dialogue, we assemble these essays for you to think with as you study the New Testament. In doing so, we thank Carey C. Newman, at the time Senior Editor, Academic Books, at Westminster John Knox Press and now Director of Church Relations, Office of the President, Baylor University, for conceiving of this project, for asking us to do it, and for shepherding it through the publication process.

To Krister Stendahl, we dedicate these pages with deepest appreciation and thanks for providing all of us with such a model of intellectual and moral integrity in this highly charged and delicate enterprise of enhancing Jewish-Christian understanding. Lutheran pastor, biblical scholar, Harvard professor, bishop of Stockholm in his native Sweden, Krister has been a constant and tireless worker in the vineyard of Christian-Jewish dialogue for half a century.

Before audiences of all different denominations, he has continually called on Christians *as* Christians to renounce the contempt for Judaism that has haunted and at times utterly compromised the church's mission of peace. As a scholar, he has published seminal essays on the Gospel of Matthew and—especially befitting a Lutheran theologian—on Paul's letters, particularly the Epistle to the Romans. As a professor, he stands as an important academic parent to many of us in the intergenerational community of teachers and students in North America.

But it is as a pastor that Krister has most succinctly put the point that brings us—authors and readers—together here. Pondering Paul's way of reading Scripture, Krister once observed, "In the very text that comes to us through tradition lies the very truth that criticizes that tradition."[1] Krister was referring to Romans 10:6–9:

> But the righteousness that comes from faith says, "Do not say in your heart, 'Who will ascend into heaven?'" (that is, to bring Christ down) "or 'Who will descend into the abyss?'" (that is, to bring Christ up from the dead). But what does it say? "The word is near you, on your lips and in your heart" (that is, the word of faith that we proclaim); because if you confess with your lips that Jesus is Lord and believe in your heart that God raised him from the dead, you will be saved.[2]

In this passage, Paul alluded to Deuteronomy 30:11-14 (Deuteronomy is the repetition and summary that closes Israel's core canon, the Torah, or the five books of Moses):

> Surely, this commandment that I am commanding you today is not too hard for you, nor is it too far away. It is not in heaven, that you should say, "Who will go up to heaven for us, and get it for us so that we may hear it and observe it?" Neither is it beyond the sea, that you should say, "Who will cross to the other side of the sea for us, and get it for us so that we may hear it and observe it?" No, the word is very near to you; it is in your mouth and in your heart for you to observe.

The truth that Paul saw, which defined his call to be an apostle, was that the redemption of Gentiles in Christ cohered deeply with the teachings of Torah. A preacher might say, as Paul did, that Gentile branches had been grafted onto the Jewish tree but that the Jewish tree remains. Think otherwise, Paul warned his Gentile readers in Rome, and you distort the essential message of the gospel.

The text Krister holds in mind is Romans, and the larger canon of the New Testament. The truth that he sees is that the tradition of Christian contempt for Judaism, commonly understood to be taught by the New Testament texts, is challenged and repudiated by those very same texts. Think otherwise, Krister has warned his modern listeners, and you distort the gospel.

It is our hope that this volume will help others to grapple with the difficult issue of Christian anti-Judaism and thereby further the important mission to which Krister has dedicated himself for so many years.

NOTES

1. Krister Stendahl, *Final Accounts, or, Paul's Letter to the Romans* (Minneapolis: Fortress Press, 1995), p. 35.
2. All biblical texts are quoted from the New Revised Standard Version (1989) unless otherwise noted.

1

The Birth of Christianity and the Origins of Christian Anti-Judaism

Paula Fredriksen

Jesus of Nazareth was a Jew. The crowds who heard him, his earliest disciples, the apostle Paul—all were Jews. The holy days and sacred writings of the earliest community were the festivals and Scriptures of Israel. Yet, as it grew, Christianity became a community conspicuous for *not* living according to Jewish law and tradition. Gentiles, not Jews, dominated the movement. As a religion, Christianity came to be defined—and, indeed, defined itself—by its hostility toward Jews and Judaism.

How did this happen? And when did it happen? To try to grasp the answers, we need to begin at the beginning—which, in turn, brings us to yet another question: When does Christianity begin?

Before we can even start our inquiry, we have to define the object of our search, and decide what we mean by "Christianity." If we mean the religious community that worships the Triune God and that acknowledges Jesus Christ as fully God and fully man, then we would place its beginnings sometime in the fourth century. That would be a good answer, because by the fourth century so much of what would characterize Christianity for the next sixteen hundred years was finally in place: powerful bishops, great councils, and a philosophically sophisticated theology that could insist on both three-ness and unity in the Godhead. By the fourth century, the church recognized and patronized by the Roman emperor was an international Gentile community hostile to diversity both within and without: Christians outside the officially sanctioned church were persecuted as heretics; pagan nonparticipants increasingly became the object of legal harassment; Jews, though permitted their peculiar worship, were universally condemned as enemies of the prophets and murderers of Christ.

When we turn to the New Testament, however, a different and obvious answer presents itself: Christianity begins with Jesus of Nazareth and continues through his apostle, Paul. Many of the themes that define fourth-century Christian orthodoxy seem already present in the Christian canon. The high Christology (theology of Christ) of Nicaea is no more elevated than the claims made for Christ in the Gospel of John. "The Father and I are one," teaches John's Jesus (John 10:30); and the disciple Thomas exclaims before the risen Christ, "My Lord and my God!" (20:28). As for heresy, in the Synoptic Gospels—Matthew, Mark, and Luke—Jesus seems already to condemn some Christians as deviants. He warns against false insiders in the course of his Sermon on the Mount, cautioning his flock about supposed prophets "who come to you in sheep's clothing but inwardly are ravenous wolves" (Matt. 7:15). On the last day, such so-called Christians will get their just reward:

> Not every one who says to me, "Lord, Lord," will enter the kingdom of heaven, but only the one who does the will of my Father in heaven. On that day many will say to me, "Lord, Lord, did we not prophesy in your name, and cast out demons in your name, and do many deeds of power in your name?" Then I will declare to them, "I never knew you; go away from me, you evildoers." (Matt. 7:21–23)

Paganism too is condemned, implicitly by Jesus, explicitly by Paul. The first commandment of all, Jesus instructs, is "The Lord our God, the Lord is one" (Mark 12:29): one Lord cannot admit of many. Paul, teaching to Gentiles who are former pagans, is more direct. "You turned to God from idols," he tells his community in Thessalonica, "to serve a living and true God" (1 Thess. 1:9). "Formerly, when you did not know God, you were enslaved to beings that by nature are not gods," he reminds his congregations in Galatia (Gal. 4:8). If one of his Gentiles-in-Christ slips back into idol worship, he is to be shunned by the rest of the church: "Do not even eat with such a one" (1 Cor. 5:11). Those who still worship idols are given up to futility, perversion, and death (Rom. 1:18–32). As for Judaism, Jesus and Paul speak with one voice: it is condemned. Repudiating the Pharisees and scribes, Jesus condemns the Jewish observance of the Sabbath, the food laws, and blood sacrifices, while Paul renounces circumcision, and associates Jewish law with the evil power of flesh and death.

The views just summarized once described opinions that churches and theological faculties held in common. But about two centuries ago, academic opinion began to shift as scholars started to apply the standards of developing scientific historical research to the New Testament, investigating it as they would any other ancient document. In consequence, the differences in tone and content among the Gospels emerged with increasing clarity, which in turn called into question their status as historical witnesses to the life and times of

Jesus. The evangelists in their individuality came to be seen more as creative interpreters of traditions from and about Jesus, and thus as witnesses first of all to their own communities and their own historical periods, rather than as historical witnesses to Jesus of Nazareth, who had lived and preached (in Aramaic, not in Greek) some forty to seventy years prior to these Gospels' composition. This linguistic gap between Jesus and the earliest documents about him highlighted another difference between him and later Christian tradition that was very significant theologically: Jesus would have been familiar with Semitic-language versions of the Jewish Bible (whether Hebrew or Aramaic), whereas Paul and the evangelists all drew on its Greek version, the Septuagint. Where these two biblical traditions diverged sharply—say, in the rendering of Isaiah 7:14, where in the Hebrew a "young girl" (*'aalmah*) gives birth to a child, but in Greek the new mother is a "virgin" (*parthenos*)—scholars hesitated to attribute to the historical Jesus what would have been possible, so to speak, only in Greek. The gap between history and theology began to widen.

The recovery of ancient manuscripts, a project initiated during the Renaissance, also complicated research. The good news was that more copies existed of the various canonical Christian writings than of any other Greek writings from antiquity (including those of Homer, Plato, or Sophocles). The bad news was that this superabundance of copies in effect eroded readers' confidence that they could know the original wording and contents of the biblical texts themselves. Each newly discovered manuscript or portion thereof brought with it another way to read a word or phrase or passage, and in this way innumerable textual variants accrued. Given the long history of the New Testament's transmission, no modern version of the text could ever be identical to whatever the original had been: too many generations of copyists stood between the scholar and the text's distant, ancient author.

Further, the discovery of buried libraries—most dramatically, in the midtwentieth century, the Dead Sea Scrolls in Israel and the Nag Hammadi library in Egypt—increased scholarly awareness of the great variety within both ancient religious communities, Jewish and Christian. The best-known forms of each tradition, rabbinic Judaism on the one hand and Catholic orthodoxy on the other, had dominated the historical record—and therefore the historical imagination—in no small part because their great literary legacies were virtually the sole ones to have survived from antiquity. The texts of their respective competition, history's losers—Sadducees, Essenes, Hellenistic Jews; or Gnostic, Jewish, or millenarian Christians—had been suppressed, destroyed, or lost. But the two victorious communities had definitively established themselves only in the fourth century. To see their own definitions of their respective traditions as *the* standard or normative versions for any earlier period was anachronistic and, thus, distorting. Some historians, in light of this realization, conjectured that the earliest forms of Christianity known in different parts of the Empire might well have been seen as heretical only in subsequent periods. Any absolute value to the concept of orthodoxy, in other words, evaporated. This, in turn, raised the question: Absent orthodoxy for the period before Constantine, what was the relation of Christian theology to its own origins, and where should those origins be sought?

Finally, as historians worked to reconstruct critically from ancient evidence the figures both of Jesus and of Paul in their respective religious and cultural environments, two issues grew increasingly clear: the importance of Jewish apocalyptic traditions as a religious orientation, and the importance of Greek-speaking synagogue communities in the Diaspora as a social matrix for Jewish-Gentile interaction.

Throughout the nineteenth century, scholars seeking the historical Jesus had struggled with the meaning of the key phrase frequently on his lips in the Synoptic Gospels, the "kingdom of God." As long as the phrase could be seen as some kind of moral metaphor—by invoking the kingdom of God, Jesus really meant to say, "Love one another," or "Feed the hungry," or "Be kind to widows and orphans"—Jesus could be looked at primarily as a teacher of elevated ethics. Of course, an ethic of love and compassion is as effortlessly meaningful to moderns as to ancients. The liberal Protestant scholars who were then at the forefront of historical Jesus work saw Jesus precisely and primarily in this ethical mode. Thus, in preaching the kingdom of God, the great scholar Adolf von Harnack explained, Jesus was actually teaching "the fatherhood of God and the brotherhood of man." Such a reconstruction of Jesus' message took the prophetic writings of the Old Testament as the prime interpretive context for Jesus' message. In this view, Jesus was the ultimate spokesman for the great ethical tradition expressed in Isaiah and Micah and Hosea that emphasized righteousness and love, justice and mercy. This ethical stance (so went the argument) stood in stark contrast to the Temple cult, the "works of the law," and other such Jewish "distortions" of biblical tradition. Jesus' core message, in other words, happened to coincide exactly with the way that later (Gentile) Christianity saw and defined itself against what it perceived Judaism to be. This way of thinking restated as a seeming principle of doing history what was in fact basic to the structure of the Christian canon itself, wherein the gospel completes the Law and the Prophets, and the New Testament succeeds the "Old."

Scholars next began branching out of canonical Jewish writings into those much less familiar ones written in the period that fell roughly between the Maccabees and the Mishnah, from 200 B.C.E. to 200 C.E., which scholars referred to as the "intertestamental period." These writings, too, interpreted Jewish classical prophecy. Not infrequently, they too spoke of a coming kingdom of

God. But in these texts, it was clear, the kingdom was no timeless moral metaphor. It named a longed-for, energetically anticipated historical event. When the kingdom came, the God of Israel would reveal himself in glory. The righteous might at first be in travail (*Assumption of Moses*), but ultimately they would triumph, perhaps under the human leadership of an anointed leader, the Lord's messiah (*Baruch*). The dead would rise (*Daniel*), the scattered tribes of Israel would be gathered in from exile and reassembled in a renewed and resplendent Jerusalem (*Enoch; Tobit*). Perhaps one like a Son of Man would appear to judge the quick and the dead (*Enoch*). The Gentiles would finally abandon their idols and acknowledge Israel's God as the only God (*Isaiah; Tobit; Sybilline Oracles*). Knowledge of the Lord would radiate out from Zion to the whole earth (*Isaiah; Micah; Psalm of Solomon*). The strong theme in these intertestamental writings was apocalyptic eschatology: the conviction that God was about to intervene definitively in history, vanquish injustice, evil, and death forever, and establish his kingdom of peace.

Both thematically and chronologically, these writings stand much closer to the traditions from and about Jesus in the Gospels and in the letters of Paul than do the "Old Testament" writings as such. They thus enable us to glimpse how the canonical prophets such as Isaiah and Micah were heard and interpreted by Jews in the period just preceding and following the early Jesus movement. As scholars placed the New Testament writings within the interpretive context of these intertestamental apocalyptic ones, the apocalyptic accent of earliest Christian tradition sounded with increasing clarity. This trajectory of research culminated in the early twentieth century with Albert Schweitzer's great classic, *The Quest of the Historical Jesus* (1906). And this new emphasis on the earliest tradition's own apocalypticism in turn raised the question: If Jesus in his lifetime, and his apostles in theirs, had expected and preached the imminent arrival of this sort of divine kingdom, of what relevance was their message to the church so many long centuries after the fact? If they expected the end of normal time so long ago, how can they be thought of in any way as having *intended* to found a new religious community distinct from their native Judaism? And if they did not, then again the question arises: What is the relation of the later church to its own earliest history?

Finally, archaeological and historical work on the ancient Greco-Roman city, and the place of Greek-speaking Jewish communities within such cities, has powerfully affected the study of Christian origins. Earlier scholars, in part drawing on a particular reading of Acts, in part projecting a much later, idealized rabbinic model of separation back onto ancient Diaspora communities, had imagined Greek-speaking Jews as living apart and aloof from their pagan Gentile neighbors. Such supposed aloofness was in turn seen as the cause of the Greco-Roman anti-Semitism visible in certain Hellenistic and Latin authors. According to this view, Jewish separatism provoked pagan anti-Semitism. Such supposed Jewish self-segregation in turn underscored the dramatic novelty of ancient Christianity, wherein Paul and the other apostles to the Gentiles were seen as accomplishing the unprecedented: dissolving the barriers between Gentile and Jew; bringing knowledge of biblical religion to Gentile populations; creating the circumstances in which, for the first time, Jew and Gentile might together worship the God of Israel without any pressure on the Gentiles actually to convert to Judaism and thus to keep Jewish law.

Recent work on archaeological remains, especially inscriptions, as well as on various sorts of ancient literature have altered this picture fundamentally. It now seems clear that, by the dawn of the Roman Empire, synagogue communities had long been a familiar fixture on the Mediterranean urban landscape. Much of ancient religious practice was communal and outdoors, and Jewish Diaspora religious practice was no exception to this general rule. The cultural habit of religious openness encouraged the participation of outsiders, so that Jews might be found enjoying the spectacles available in the amphitheaters, gymnasia, and civic centers of their cities of residence. These spectacles customarily began with public rituals honoring traditional deities and, eventually, the divinity of the Roman emperor: one inscription from an ancient city marked off the particular place in the stands reserved for Jewish viewers. Traffic went in the other direction too: Gentiles might be present during Jewish communal celebrations, whether on the Sabbath or other feasts, where they along with their Jewish neighbors would hear stories and instruction from the Scriptures delivered in Greek. Philo of Alexandria, in the first century, mentions the mixed crowd of Jews and Gentiles who gathered annually to celebrate the local Jewish festival commemorating the Greek translation of the Bible. Later pagan magical papyri, in their recipes for casting certain spells, relate garbled versions of biblical stories, which magicians could easily have obtained by dropping in at the synagogue.

Diaspora Jews permitted and even encouraged sympathetic Gentiles to contribute more directly to synagogue life. Jewish donor inscriptions honor prominent local pagans—here a priestess of the imperial cult, there a town councillor—for their patronage in constructing, refurbishing, or beautifying synagogue buildings or contributing to Jewish charities. The huge and beautiful remains of the fourth-century synagogue at Sardis shows a Jewish house of worship literally at the heart of this ancient city, structurally integrated into the same architectural complex that housed the baths and the marketplace. One of the city's public fountains stood in its forecourt. This was no segregated community. Some sympathetic pagans even went so far as to adopt voluntarily some Jewish customs such as keeping the Sabbath, or the food laws, or observing other Jewish holidays, thereby annoying pagan writers like Juvenal and Tacitus.

These pagan Judaizers, called "God-fearers" in Greek sources (*theosobeis* or *sebomenoi*), "fearers of heaven" in Hebrew (*yirei shamayim*), could be found in cities throughout the Empire, wherever a Jewish community lived.

We should pause to consider these voluntary Judaizers, because their existence tells us much both about pagan culture and about Jewish culture. Pagan culture itself was religiously pluralistic. Ancient peoples typically worshiped their own ancestral gods—in antiquity, religion ran in the blood—and these gods formed aggregates of larger pantheons as politics required. (When Alexander the Great conquered Egypt in the fourth century B.C.E., for example, he identified a chief Egyptian sky god, Amon, with the Greek's chief sky god, Zeus. Alexander himself, once divinized, was worshiped as the divine son of Amon-Zeus.) Further, simple courtesy and common sense encouraged showing respect to gods as they were encountered. Pagan interest in the Jewish god was thus one particular instance of the general pagan interest in any divinity. And Jews, a minority wherever they lived in the Diaspora, encouraged this sympathetic interest in their own God, while making no demands on the volunteer. Thus, in the innumerable synagogues scattered throughout the Empire, Jews made room for pagans, as pagans, to worship the God of Israel, just as in Jerusalem's great Temple, until its destruction in 70 C.E., the largest court was set aside for pagans to worship the Jewish God.

Those pagans who chose to Judaize, that is, to assume observance of some Jewish customs, did so on an individual, voluntary, ad hoc, and improvised basis. Other pagans complained of such Judaizing not so much because of the practices themselves—holy days, food protocols, and concerns with purity were native to all ancient religions, not just to Judaism—but because such Judaizing might and evidently did occasionally lead to conversion. Converts to Judaism by definition changed their status from sympathetic outsider to committed insider; for men, in addition, this meant being circumcised, a procedure regarded with revulsion by the majority culture. For any convert, male or female, conversion to Judaism required abstention from traditional worship. Becoming a Jew, in effect, meant changing ethnicity, choosing new ancestors; choosing Jewish ancestors meant renouncing one's own gods.

In other words, though Diaspora Judaism was inclusive with respect to outsiders, whose sympathetic involvement was encouraged, it was exclusive with respect to insiders: Jews in principle were forbidden foreign gods. Jewish religious exclusivism made life complicated enough for born Jews. Josephus gives ample evidence of the various concessions that Jews living abroad had to wrangle from civic authorities, such as permission not to appear in court on the Sabbath or another holy day, and exemption from public rites when offering testimony in court. One community had to petition authorities to set aside a certain number of animals not to be sacrificed to the gods so that resident Jews could have access to meat uncontaminated by idolatry. (Echoes of this last concern show up in Paul's letters.) Some hostile pagan observers considered this exclusivism—which in the pre-Christian period was unique to Judaism—to be rude, if not downright seditious. Thus conversion to Judaism, for the formerly pagan convert, had immediate and serious social consequences, especially in light of the public nature of ancient religion: to take on Jewish exclusivism by choosing to convert wrested Gentiles out of their own culture and their own habitual patterns of participation in their own city. Nonetheless, pagan civic and imperial authorities by and large granted Jews the exemptions from civic cult that they sought out of respect for their *patria ethē*, the ethnicity and antiquity of Jewish ancestral law. Remarkably, this pagan acknowledgment of Jewish religious difference extended even to the point of honoring the special status of former pagans who, as converts to Judaism, sought the same rights and exemptions as "native" Jews.

By the same token, most Jewish communities probably avoided deliberate outreach to pagan neighbors with the specific intention of turning them into Jews, that is, converting them to Judaism. The effect of any such missionary outreach would have been to alienate these neighbors from their own gods, families, traditions, and culture, impugning the *patria ethē* of the host culture. To upset the religious and political ecosystem of the city in this way would have endangered the Jewish community itself. Instead, it seems that Jews outside their own land made their peace, religiously and socially, with their non-Jewish neighbors, who were, after all, the vast majority of humankind.

What then of the ultimate fate of their Gentile neighbors whose lives were so mired in the worship of false gods? Those Jews who worried about such things had prophetic apocalyptic tradition to draw on, according to which, at the end of time, through the display of his majesty, God would finally turn his pagan children to himself. The belief that Gentiles would in this way be "saved" was widespread enough to find expression in the *Alenu*, an ancient prayer that expressed the hope of seeing the false gods exterminated and all humanity (*kol benei basar*, "all the children of the flesh"), Jews and Gentiles, united in the worship of the God of Israel.

This Jewish inclusiveness toward outsiders was virtually the obverse of the Jews' attitude toward each other. Extremely tolerant of those outside the fold, Jews were rancorously, almost exuberantly, intolerant of variety within the fold. Battling with each other over the correct way to be Jewish was (one could say, is) a timeless Jewish activity, and at no time more so than in the late Second Temple period, precisely the lifetime of Jesus and of Paul. This last fact must be borne in mind if we are to understand the import of those bitter polemics against scribes, Pharisees, Sadducees, and publicans attributed to Jesus in the Gospels, and the startlingly belligerent remarks against fellow apostles and other Jews that we find in Paul. In terms of the business of being Jewish, especially in the first half of the first century, such remarks are entirely normal. Indeed, when compared to some of the vituperation lavished on other sorts of Jews by the Dead Sea sectarians, these partisan statements seem rather mild.

The vivid and vital level of controversy among Jews about Judaism was the measure, and in some sense the consequence, of how widespread Jewish knowledge of Jewish Scripture was. "Should any of our nation be questioned about the laws," claimed Josephus, "he would repeat them all the more readily than his own name." Josephus probably exaggerates, but the point he makes is an interesting one. Because of the institution of weekly community gatherings on the Sabbath, Jews everywhere constituted a textual community of a special sort. By the simple expedient of reading the law aloud, synagogues, whether in the Diaspora or in the homeland, diminished both the need for literacy and the monopoly on interpretation that a literate elite might have exercised. Thus the individual Jew did not have to be literate in order to be involved in the interpretation of Scripture: Hearing the law at least once a week, completing the cycle of the Torah time and time again throughout one's life, provided text enough. The Bible, through the Jewish habit of weekly community study, permitted the growth of a secondary sort of literacy, whereby many Jews could be very familiar with a text without necessarily being able to read. (For all we know, this might have been Jesus' circumstance.) This secondary literacy in turn encouraged and intensified community life: any Jew could have his or her own opinions on the correct understanding of God's Word.

The vehement, interminable debate that so marks intra-Jewish relations attests not only to how widespread knowledge of the Bible was, but also to how seriously performance of its dictates was regarded. At stake was not *whether* the law should be observed—quarreling implies unanimity on this point—but *how*. Precisely this point is made in the Gospels' various controversy stories: the Pharisees maintain that a law (honoring the Sabbath, say, or offering at the Temple) is to be fulfilled in one manner; Jesus argues, in another. Neither says that the command is unimportant. At issue is the way to fulfill it.

Did anything like these controversies ever actually happen? The evangelists' presentation of some of them can be flagrantly contrived. Pharisees did not routinely spend their Sabbaths patrolling grainfields (Mark 2:23–24), nor does teaching that man cannot be defiled by external things (Mark 7:19b) mean the same thing as "Don't bother keeping kosher." But the general impression that the controversy stories convey is entirely plausible. Arguing about the correct way to understand the Bible, to fulfill God's laws, in short, to be Jewish, was one of the most typical ways that religious Jews in Jesus' age lived out their commitment to Judaism.

So also with Paul's letters. His negative remarks about circumcision are motivated entirely by his position on the question of whether it should be required of Gentiles-in-Christ. This question would have been much more pressing in the Diaspora than in the overwhelmingly Jewish setting of Jesus' mission in Galilee, Samaria, and Judea. These particular Gentiles, again according to Paul's letters, had already forsaken their idols and made an *exclusive* commitment to "a living and true God" (1 Thess. 1:9)—a decision, to repeat, that the Hellenistic synagogue never demanded of them. Why then, argued Paul, should they also convert to Judaism?

Paul certainly thought that they should not convert, and he did not hesitate to say that his Christian apostolic colleagues who thought otherwise were wrong. But the issue of circumcision *for Jews* was another matter. Circumcision was one of the defining privileges of Israel, part and parcel with the divine giving of the Torah and the other special dignities that God had bestowed uniquely on his "son", the Jewish people. "They are Israelites," Paul explains in Romans, "and to them belong the sonship, the *glory*, the covenants, the giving of the law, the *worship*, and the promises; to them belong the patriarchs, and of their race, according to the flesh, is the Christ. God who is over all be blessed for ever. Amen" (9:4–5 RSV, emphasis mine). The English translation of the words that I give here in italics blankets their very important and telling connotations. "Glory," in Greek *doxa*, rests in the context of Romans 9 on the Hebrew *kavod*. in Paul's "Jewish Greek," this word immediately recalls the altar of the Temple, which Paul's native religion regarded as the earthly abode of God's presence. We see this thought in the Gospels, too, when Matthew's Jesus says, "Whoever swears by the sanctuary, swears by it and by the one who dwells in it" (23:21). "Worship" disguises another "Temple" word: the Greek *latreia* translates the Hebrew *avodah*, meaning specifically, again in Paul's Jewish Greek, the cult of animal sacrifice mandated in the Torah and performed before God's presence in Jerusalem. In sum: To extrapolate from Paul's condemnation of circumcision for Gentiles-in-Christ a condemnation of Judaism in general completely misses his point.

Indeed, the targets of Paul's most intemperate invective—with the rhetorically lush exception of his resounding condemnation of Gentile culture in toto given in the first chapter of Romans—are almost invariably other Jews. Most often, the Jews he repudiates are even closer to him and his own highly individual beliefs than we realize: not Jews in general, nor even fellow Pharisees in particular, but rather and most specifically other Jews like himself who were also preaching salvation in Christ to Gentiles. These fellow Jews are the "false apostles" and the "deceitful workers" against whom Paul fulminates (2 Cor. 11:13). And the contest is conducted in particularly Jewish terms. Whose background was unimpeachable? Paul's was, he informs his Philippian audience: he was born of Jewish parents, of the tribe of Benjamin, and circumcised when eight days old. Whose education and, thus, scriptural orientation was most sound? Again, of course, Paul's. (Hence his proclaiming himself a Pharisee "as to the law.") Whose level of religious observance was most praiseworthy? On this score, Paul claims modestly, he was "blameless" (Phil. 3:4–6). Who was most dedicated to the mission? Paul was. (For more examples of Pauline modesty, see 1 Cor. 15: 10 and 2 Cor. 11:23.) Whose teaching, then, was more authoritative? Obviously, Paul's. Any missionary with a different message—even if he were an angel!—is simply accursed (Gal. 1:8). Strong language, yes. But in the area of debate about correct religious behavior, all this is Jewish business as usual.

The core canon of the New Testament, in other words the Gospels and the letters of Paul, witness to that moment in the evolution of Christianity when it was still a type of Second Temple Judaism. The heated polemic against different types of Jews that they contain is exactly the measure of their Jewishness. But this polemic came to be read, understood, and used as a blanket condemnation of Judaism itself. By whom? Why? How? If we can answer these questions, we can glimpse the beginnings of Christianity as its own entity, a new, Gentile religion, distinct from and even antipathetic to Judaism. To do this, we must seek out the origins, specifically, of Christian theology.

Theos is Greek for "god." *Logos* is Greek for "order, reason, word." Theology is systematic, ordered discourse on the nature of divinity. As such, theology was not native to ancient religion, whether pagan or Jewish.

To the pagans first. The term "paganism" itself gives a false impression, because any "ism" presupposes some sort of organized thought. Paganism sounds like a body of doctrine, standing in contrast to Christianity, which had a different doctrine. The word in fact was a fourth-century Christian neologism, a derogatory term contrived by the victorious church to describe that part of the Empire's population—probably in that period still the majority—which was neither Jewish nor Christian. The phenomenon it signifies is the innumerable traditional, indigenous polytheisms of the ancient world. These defined themselves much more in terms of local and inherited practices (which varied, and were never systematically coordinated) than in terms of formal beliefs.

Ancient Judaism, too, for the most part lacked theology. God in the Bible is not the subject of systematic reflection, but another character in the narrative. He creates and he blesses; he forgets and then remembers; he has his enthusiasms, his disappointments, and his triumphs. God's *nature* in the Bible is communicated through story, or by simple declaration. ("You are a gracious

God," complains Jonah at 4:2, embarrassed when repentant Nineveh is spared ruin. "[You are] merciful, slow to anger, and abounding in steadfast love, and ready to relent from punishing.") Divine nature in the Bible is not the object of systematic investigation or abstract thought, nor are God's characteristics arrived at through a process of logical reasoning.

Theology began not in temples or around altars, but in the ancient academy. It was, in this sense, a secular subject, a special branch of philosophy, and philosophy was quite distinct from traditional Greek cult. The ways in which philosophers conceived the nature of divinity coordinated with their views on the nature of matter, time, nature, the soul, reason, and so on. God was part of a larger, ideally coordinated and rational system.

In the late fourth century B.C.E., these Greek intellectual ways of thinking began to be exported on a grand scale, thanks to the conquests of Alexander the Great. In consequence of his victories, in part as a deliberate policy of acculturation, he established Greek cities throughout his newly acquired territories, from Egypt and Asia Minor throughout the Middle East to the edges of Persia. Greek spread as an international language. An international form of Greek culture, called "Hellenism," was disseminated precisely through the social and physical structures of these new cities which, like the classical city that they interpreted and took as a model, contained the major organs for preserving and expressing that culture. These included the agora (a central public space, the commercial and social nerve center of the city), the civic temples (at whose altars animals for public feasts would be offered to the gods), the school (for primary education), the gymnasium (a public educational center first of all for adolescent male citizens, which taught literature, music, and mathematics and philosophy as well as athletics), the public library, a space for meetings of the boulē or town council, and perhaps a theater or amphitheater or hippodrome. Once Rome conquered the Greek world in the second century B.C.E., it adapted itself to Hellenistic culture too. Romans too built cities with public temples, libraries, baths, town councils, and theaters throughout the huge sweep of its westward territories: North Africa, the Iberian peninsula, Britain, France, and Germany.

As a result, educated urban elites from one end of the Roman world to the other shared a common culture mediated by gymnasium education. The curriculum for these young men was universal, and exceedingly stable: from one century to the next, they would be taught the great epic poets and the tragedians, modes of public speaking derived from classical models, music, philosophy. This high-cultural mix of rhetorical and philosophical culture was called *paideia*.

Philosophical thought (especially in those forms that owed most to Plato) complicated traditional religiousness in interesting ways. The revered ancient poems and dramas that conveyed the gripping myths and stories of the adventures of gods and men clashed directly with philosophical modes of conceiving divinity. The curriculum of the gymnasium saturated young men with both the mythological and the philosophical literatures. The principles of paideia organized reality on a continuum that expressed tensions between its extreme ends. Matter, for example—mutable, gross, intellectually inert, perceptible by the senses—contrasted with spirit, which was thought of as matter's opposite: eternal, nonmaterial, rational, perceptible only through the mind or reason, the "god" or divine principle or "eye" of the soul. To see matter as "bad" since spirit, clearly, was "good," was a temptation inherent in the Platonic system itself, one that many Platonists strenuously attempted to avoid.

The physical cosmos (Greek) or universe (Latin) expressed through the very fact of its organization a sort of negotiated settlement between these two extremes. Here matter existed with form, thus expressing or in a sense reflecting the beauty and order of its superior, the divine realm. But according to philosophy, the highest god, the ultimate cause of everything else, radically transcended even the more perfect, more beautiful parts of cosmos, such as the heavens and the realm of the fixed stars. This highest being—also referred to as the One, the Being, the Father—was absolutely, radically stable, free of body of any sort (even of the very fine, rarefied, perfect bodies possessed by astral intelligences), impassable, eternal, unchanging. Everything else was contingent or dependent on him, in the sense that he or it was its ultimate source.

Still, and it is extremely important to hold this thought in mind, the High God, though the ultimate source of everything else, was in no sense its "creator." Creating or even ordering, indeed any sort of "making" or "doing," would have at least implicitly involved the One in time and change. Worse: both ethically and metaphysically, it would have implicated God, the ultimate Good, in the problem of evil, given the rank imperfections of the physical universe, especially in that realm where earth stood, below the moon. Thus in pagan systems, as eventually in Jewish and Christian ones, divine intermediaries, such as a demiurge ("craftsman") or Logos (a personification of divine creative intelligence) or angels did the job.

How, then, could thinkers of good education reconcile the culturally revered depictions of divinities that they read in Homer or Hesiod—wherein gods bred, brawled, raped, cannibalized their own offspring, and in general behaved in ways one would not tolerate in humans—with the theological principles conveyed through paideia? Through allegory. The ancient myths could be enjoyed and appreciated as the terrific adventure stories they were. If contemplated for religious significance, however, and thus related to the categories of theology, they had to be understood at a deeper, or spiritual, level as narrative symbols for metaphysical truths. Thus, for example, the story of Zeus turning himself into an eagle in order to seize the beautiful boy Ganymede could be understood allegorically as a description of the rapture felt by the soul when it is seized and carried "upward" by its intellectual contemplation of the One.

The philosophically educated were *not* atheists. They were not, in their intellectual allegiance to paideia, denying that the traditional gods existed or that their worship was important. Indeed, precisely this class of men populated the councils of cities throughout the Empire, and thus as part of their municipal responsibilities they financially underwrote and publically celebrated, with games, animal slaughter, and public feasting, the traditional cults of these gods. But seen from the perspective of philosophy, divinity, like the physical universe that in some ways reflected it, was organized as a hierarchy. The perfection of physical body and rational intelligence (according to ancient astronomical science as well as paideia) was visibly evident in the Milky Way, the luminous and immortal band of astral beings at the edge of the universe, which were thought to have independent life. The lowest levels of matter and intelligence (as was plainly observable in everyday life) were sunk at the universe's bottom or center, the earth. So too divinity stood in ranks from lowest to highest, from the familiar sublunar beings, the demons and family and local gods that lived close at hand, to the higher gods of the classical pantheon who dwelt in and directed the heavens, and finally, at the apex of reality, to the purely spiritual, absolutely perfect and unchanging Father, the One.

Those pagans who thought in these terms may properly be thought of as monotheists, because for them everything else, including lower deities, devolved from a single, highest god. In exactly the same way, ancient Jews and, eventually, Christians may also be said to be monotheists. These last two groups certainly did not deny the existence of the pagan gods; rather, they denied their power and moral status relative to that of the Highest God, whom these two later groups identified with the god whom they worshiped. Alternatively, they dismissed the pagan gods as malevolent powers or demons. But for all three groups—pagans, Jews, and Christians—the lower gods were real.

Hellenism affected Jewish culture profoundly. Jews living in the Hellenistic cities of the Mediterranean Diaspora absorbed Greek as their vernacular, as the very existence of the Septuagint attests. They also lived within the god-drenched environment of these cities. They thus had to make their peace with the gods of these other nations, around whose cult pulsed their city's social and religious life. Jews did not deny that these gods existed. Rather they avoided involving themselves in pagan worship, particularly if they wanted to be traditionally pious. How this worked out—what constituted involvement—

undoubtedly varied among individuals within a single community, and across Jewish communities within different cities. Young Jewish men in Egypt, for example, gained access to a gymnasium education, and thus joined the ranks of the city's *ephebes*, the name for these adolescent males. How do we know this? Because Jewish names appear in inscriptions among those listed as members of the ephebate. But ephebes had municipal obligations. They would sing hymns to the gods or compete in athletic competitions as part of some civic activities. Such festivals invariably involved sacrifices and communal feasting. How did Jewish ephebes manage? Did they sing hymns to their city's gods, while telling themselves that they did not "mean" what they sang? Did they stand around the city's altars, but not eat during the meal? Would they eat during the meal, but bring their own food from home, or eat only bread or fruit, and avoid, also, the wine? We don't and can't know. I suspect that behavior varied.

Intellectual, classically educated Greek-speaking Jews also applied the principles of paideia when interpreting their own most sacred text, the Bible. They were aided in this effort by the fact that the text, by the end of the second century B.C.E., existed in Greek translation. But the descriptions of the god of the Septuagint were no more philosophically acceptable than the descriptions of divinity in Homer. The first sentence of the entire collection, if understood literally, got things off on the wrong foot by proclaiming, "In the beginning God made . . . ." Either the creator god doing the making was not the Highest God, or, if he were, then the word "making" had to be interpreted allegorically. In the numerous commentaries of the learned first-century Jewish philosopher Philo of Alexandria, the biblical stories about God transmute into allegories relating philosophical truths through the application of paideia's interpretive principles. Thus it is within the erudite, literate streams of Hellenistic Jewish culture that we find, for the first time, what might properly be called a biblical theology.

By the early second century C.E., the penetration of the Christian message into the educated classes of the Hellenistic world becomes evident by the types of learned intra-Christian disputes that we glimpse in our sources. Formerly pagan Gentile intellectuals who converted to Christianity took on the relatively recent revelation attributable to Jesus. In so doing, they struggled with an intensified form of the same problem that troubled educated Jews about the depictions of God in the Septuagint, and that troubled educated pagans about the texts of their cultural canon (Homer, Hesiod, and so on). Theology in all three modes, Christian, Jewish, and pagan, was the varied expression of a more general intellectual struggle to make philosophical sense of religion. In the case of Christianity, however, the struggle was additionally complicated by the fact that Christians had no sacred Scriptures of their own. Paul's letters and the gospels (many more gospels than would ultimately be preserved in the early third-century anthology known to us as the New Testament), various apocalypses and revelations, and a rich assortment of pseudonymous epistles all circulated widely; but these texts did not have the status of sacred scripture. For most Christian communities, throughout most of the second century, the only Bible was the Jews' Bible, the Septuagint. This simple fact ultimately had enormous theological and social consequences for both groups—and for pagans as well.

One of the earliest Christian theologians whose name we know was Valentinus (fl. 130 C.E.). As a Christian who believed that the knowledge of salvation came through Jesus Christ, and as an intellectual imbued with the principles of paideia, Valentinus attempted to make systematic, religious sense of the Septuagint. He did so by reading it, so to speak, in reverse. Clearly, decided Valentinus, the god who appeared in the opening chapters of Genesis was not the Highest God, precisely because he was involved in material creation. (Philo, earlier, had finessed this problem by attributing the actual work to God's Logos and his angels.) Further, this god was an ignorant god, which also enunciated his lower status: He could not find Adam when he went looking for him, but had to call out to him, and he did not know what had transpired in the garden until he asked (Gen. 3:9, 13). Further, he was not good, but malevolent. What else could explain his desire to keep Adam and Eve from the knowledge of good and evil? And so, Valentinus concluded, the two real heroes of the story were the serpent and Eve.

The god of Genesis, Valentinus argued, was a low, jealous deity of the material cosmos. What could the relationship of such a god possibly be to the Lord Jesus Christ? Here philosophy's prejudices against the status of matter—it was inferior to spirit, in some sense its opposite metaphysically and thus, perhaps, morally—combined with the way that Valentinus, and gnostic ("knowing") Christians generally, interpreted the Christian message and understood the Septuagint's relationship to the Jews. Jesus, they maintained, had been sent into this lower material cosmos by his Father, the true High God. To accomplish his mission, Jesus appeared in the likeness of flesh, in the form of a human being (cf. Phil. 2:7–8). But of course he had not actually had a physical body, because matter was the evil medium of the evil lower god. It was this lower god, the god of Genesis, who was Jesus' dire opponent. The Jews, entangled in myriad fleshly customs (like circumcision, and endless fussing about what to eat), in their error confused this creator with the High God. But the Christian knew better, Valentinus maintained. He could read the Jews' book as the coded revelation of Christ that it actually was, because he had the *gnōsis* ("knowledge") to interpret it aright, *kata pneuma*, as Paul said, with "spiritual knowledge." Only some of Scripture's laws were from the lower creator god of Genesis, and some were from the Jews with their endless traditions. But some, discretely, were related to Christ. Christians with the true knowledge of salvation imparted to them by Jesus—unlike carnal-minded, false, or inferior Christians, and certainly unlike the Jews—were able to see these distinctions.

Through this knowledge of salvation, the gnostic understood the universe, and how he himself, through Christ, would be saved. His physical body was not actually part of himself: it was the gross and sinful fleshly trap by which the wicked creator held his soul captive. After death, free of matter, the gnostic, like Christ, would ascend in his spiritual body to the Father (cf. 1 Cor. 15). The resurrection to eternal life, thus, was about nothing so crude as raised fleshly bodies (another unphilosophical, indeed carnal, Jewish belief!). Resurrection was eternal life before the Father, dwelling with him forever in the purely spiritual realm of the highest heaven.

Valentinus's theology was coherent and systematic. It articulated salvation in Christ in terms that made sense to the sort of morally sensitive, intellectually creative religious thinker that Valentinus was. It also made sense of the Septuagint, and in so doing defined the relation of Judaism to Christianity. In brief, the Jews had systematically misinterpreted their own book.

Another equally thoughtful, equally vibrant Christian theology was the work of a man named Marcion (fl. 140). Like Valentinus, and like many of his well-educated peers, Marcion also regarded matter as inferior, both morally and metaphysically, to spirit. Accordingly, he too held that the Highest God had nothing to do with matter; that the god whom the Jews worshiped, the god of Genesis, was a lower cosmic deity; that Christ had only seemed to have a fleshly body, but of course did not really have one; and that the Christian believer, redeemed through Christ from matter, the flesh, and sin, would pass through this material cosmos after death to the spiritual realm of the Father. But unlike Valentinus, Marcion approached the problems posed by the Septuagint differently. The letters of Paul, rather than the stories in Genesis, provided his interpretive plumb line; and this made all the difference to the subsequent history of Christianity.

Marcion took the contrasting pairs that characterized Paul's rhetoric—flesh / spirit; law/gospel; works/grace; sin/grace; circumcision, or the works of the flesh/baptism, or the works of the Spirit (remember, in this last case, that the historical Paul was concerned with Christian Gentiles being circumcised, not with circumcision as such)—and polarized what Paul had contrasted. Accordingly, he insisted that there was no relation, of any sort, between Judaism and Christianity: they too were opposites. Nothing if not consistent, Marcion then applied this principle to sacred Scripture itself. The Septuagint, as the Jews always claimed and as people generally perceived, was indeed, Marcion agreed, a Jewish book. He therefore concluded: Let the Jews have it. The new community, the church, would have its own Bible, not the "old testament" of the synagogue, but the *new* testament. By this time, the first half of the second century, there were enough specifically Christian writings in circulation to provide Marcion with good texts. He chose as the Christian canon a single gospel (we do not know which one), and the body of Paul's letters. These Marcion first "corrected," purging all the places where Paul had seemed to say something positive about Jewish law—that it was holy, and just, and good (Rom. 7:12), that it set out the standard of decent community behavior, even for Gentiles (Gal. 5:14–15), or that the Gentile in Christ should strive to keep its commandments (1 Cor. 7:19; Rom. 8:4; 13:8–10). These statements had obviously been planted in copies of the letters by Paul's enemies; Paul himself, Marcion was certain, would never have said anything positive about the law.

Both the Valentinian and the Marcionite forms of Gentile Christianity spread broadly throughout the Empire, and established long-lived and vigorous churches. When pagan cities began to persecute Gentile Christians, members of these churches were among the martyred. But there were other Gentile Christian intellectuals who did not concur with their theologies. This third group insisted on a positive relationship between material creation and the High God, between (to phrase the same principle differently) the god of Genesis and the revelation of Christ. The same god, a good god, they insisted, stood behind both the giving of the law and the establishment of the church. Their theology (as their gnostic and Marcionite opposition was quick to observe) seemed "Jewish" to the degree that they insisted that Christ had had a fleshly body, that he had indeed descended from the house of David, and that the entirety of the Septuagint, understood correctly, actually referred to Christ and his church. Christ's flesh, they further argued, did not compromise his goodness because (again like the Jews) they did not think that flesh itself was evil. Further, they urged, both Christ's resurrection and the final redemption of his saints meant that the fleshly body itself would be saved. Yet more "Jewish" still: when indeed the saints did rise, when the kingdom came in the flesh, when Christ returned also in his glorious fleshly body, then, said these Christians, Jesus and his saints would gather together and celebrate a thousand-year-long Sabbath in a renewed and resplendent Jerusalem, just as the prophets had promised.

This third Gentile Christian group thus found itself in a much more complex polemical situation than did the first two. Like Valentinus and like Marcion, so too these Christians repudiated Jewish practice, renouncing circumcision, Sabbath observance, food laws, and so on as merely "works of the flesh" unnecessary for salvation. In their view, too, these practices were wrongheaded because they were based on an unintelligent reading of the Septuagint. But in contrast to Marcion or Valentinus, these Christians held on to and prized in a positive way those Scriptures enjoining the very practices that they renounced. Their more consistent competitors held that the Bible, its god, and the Jews who valued them were fleshly, unintelligent, and wrong; this third group, on the contrary, held that the Jews alone were fleshly, unintelligent, and wrong. Understood correctly, read not for what it said but for what it meant, read in other words *kata pneuma*, with spiritual understanding, the Bible was actually a (Gentile) Christian text. Circumcision was never about foreskins and other such fleshly matters; it was a moral metaphor for circumcising the heart. Purification by immersion actually referred to baptism. The food laws were not about food: understood spiritually and allegorically, they referred rather to certain sexual practices. Hare, for example, was forbidden not because God cared about food, but because he cared about sex. Known to be sexually profligate and to shift between male and female gender itself, the hare obviously symbolized homosexuality. And so on.

The god of the Bible was likewise redeemed. These Christians, consistent with the principles of paideia, granted the Valentinians and Marcionites their point: The busy deity talking to Abraham at Mamre and to Moses at Sinai, the god who wrestled with Jacob at Jabbok, *could not* have been the High God, God the Father, the radically transcendent, serenely immutable One. It was, instead, the Father's Son, Christ before his incarnation. Christ was the god who spoke at Sinai, who spoke through Isaiah. Those Christians who thought that the Jews' law came from the lower god but that Christ came from a different source, the High God, had made a fundamental error. The lower god, the cosmic god through whom all things were made, the god who gave the law, *was* Christ himself.

So the Bible was fine (once one knew how to read it correctly), and the God of the Bible was fine (once one knew his actual identity). The problem, this third group thus maintained, was with the Jews themselves. God, through his Son, had tried to work with them, but as Moses and their own prophets had complained, they were a hard-hearted, stubborn, and carnal people. They did keep the law, but in a carnal way, interpreting it literally rather than allegorically. This accusation would have surprised Philo, who had kept the law "literally" but also allegorized it. What for Philo was a both/and situation—both keep the law according to tradition and understand it philosophically, as Moses (Philo was sure) had always intended—for these later Gentile Christians was an either/or. Either fleshly understanding or spiritual understanding, but not both. Either Jewish practice or christological allegory. In short, either Judaism or Christianity.

That the Jews did not see this themselves, said this third group of Christians, only confirmed the strength of their terrible obduracy, which their own Scriptures unendingly condemned. Some of the laws that defied allegorization had clearly been given to them as a punishment, because of this "hardness of heart." And when the prophets rebuked them, they had responded by murdering the prophets. (Here these Christians drew on what were originally Jewish pseudepigraphic writings, *The Lives of the Prophets*, wherein each prophet died a martyr's death. These texts still exist, but only in Christian recensions.) The Jews' trail of crimes stretched from their murder of the prophets to the murder of him who spoke through them, namely, Christ. Not only did the Jews (not Rome!) kill Christ; they repeatedly rejected the opportunity to repent of this crime held out to them for another forty years, until at last God definitively, publicly, and permanently rejected them. How so? By destroying their Temple, driving them into exile, and forbidding them access, forever, to Jerusalem. Yet despite all these clear signs, and the realization of Jesus' prophecy that the Temple would be thrown down, the Jews, incredibly, refused to realize the error of their ways. They still lived according to their traditions, still awaited the messiah, still refused to be converted to the Christianity that their own Scriptures plainly proclaimed and that Jesus and his apostle Paul had taught—the Christianity of this third group, the "orthodox."

This is the group, ultimately, that won. We know the names of their chief thinkers and have most of their writings: Justin Martyr, Tertullian, Irenaeus, Hippolytus. Marcion's work, by contrast, has been utterly lost; until the discovery at Nag Hammadi, so had Valentinus's. What then, in this context, does "winning" mean? It means. This was the church that, in 312, Constantine chose to patronize. It means: This is why more Christians were persecuted by the Roman Empire after 312 than before; the orthodox specifically targeted Valentinian and Marcionite churches for imperial suppression. It means: By the late fourth century, Christian emperors sent out armies to forcibly close pagan temples. (Rejecting the social model of the Diaspora synagogue, orthodox bishops instead imitated the biblical model of the prophets' destruction of Canaanite idols.) It means: Beginning in the European early Middle Ages, bishops often put local Jews in the position of having to choose between conversion or exile; in the High Middle Ages, between conversion or death.

Not all the points of second-century orthodox theology prevailed. After Constantine, for example, the orthodox church attempted to distance itself from Christian millenarianism, eventually asserting that when the final redemption came, resurrected fleshly bodies would dwell in the heavens, not on earth in Jerusalem. The anti-Judaism of their interpretive position, however, survived and flourished, becoming definitive of orthodox identity and theology. Once they established their anti-Jewish reading of the Septuagint, the orthodox easily read those documents that eventually comprised their own New Testament in the same way. Christianity's message, in their view, was especially clear. In proclaiming the gospel, Jesus had taught against Judaism. So had Paul.

History, apparently, confirmed the orthodox view. Rome indeed destroyed the Temple in Jerusalem in 70 C.E. Rome did defeat Bar Kokhba after the last Jewish revolt of 132–35. Rome did erase Jewish Jerusalem thereafter by erecting on its ruins the pagan city Aelia Capitolina. Jews were indeed "in exile" in the sense that they no longer had a country of their own. To the orthodox, the theological import of these historical events was unarguable. Indeed, they amounted to empirical proof of the truth of orthodox Christianity.

History, of course, has a way of lying in wait with surprises. The church had a bad year in 361, when Constantine's nephew, the emperor Julian, converted from the orthodox Christianity in which he had been raised to traditional Greco-Roman polytheism. Julian had had his fill of the church's proofs and decided that he would rebuild the Jews' temple in Jerusalem, in no small part to spite and to silence the bishops. (The project ran aground the following year, when Julian died on campaign.) The church had another bad year in 1897, on the eve of the first World Zionist Congress: A reconstituted state of Israel, centered around a rebuilt Jerusalem, one Jesuit spokesman averred, was flatly impossible, because it was contrary to the prediction of Christ himself. (I just want to note in passing, if this sort of thing matters to anyone, that the text of Mark 13:2 and parallels says only that all the Temple's stones will be thrown down, not that they will never again be lifted up. The passage was *read*, however, as symbolizing a permanent punishment: That is the point.) For some people 1948, when the state of Israel was established, was another tough year. So, for related reasons, was 1967, when Jerusalem was reunited under Jewish sovereignty. Is anti-Judaism, then, the same as anti-Semitism and anti-Zionism? I do not think so. The first is a theological position; the second, a racist one; the third, a political one. But, without question, the long centuries of Christianity's anti-Judaism soaked into the soil of Western culture, preparing the ground for these more recent avatars.

I opened our inquiry into early Christian-Jewish relations by posing three questions: How, given Christianity's origins in Judaism, did Christianity come to be so anti-Jewish? When did this happen? Or, to address the same issues differently: When did the form of Christianity most familiar to Western culture begin? Our narrative review of the history of this period has introduced some answers.

Christian antipathy toward Jews and Judaism began when Christian Hellenistic Jewish texts, such as the letters of Paul and the Gospels, began to circulate among total outsiders, that is, among Gentiles without any connection to the synagogue and without any attachment to Jewish traditions of practice and interpretation. At that point, the intra-Jewish polemics preserved in these texts began to be understood as condemnations of Judaism *tout court*. The next stage intensified the process, by taking this outsider's perspective to the text of the Septuagint. By the early second century, the engagement of intellectuals enriched the controversy by putting it on a philosophical basis, thereby integrating what otherwise might have remained secondhand name-calling into comprehensive, rational, total worldviews. Christian theologies of many different sorts were thereby born.

Orthodoxy's anti-Judaism was the most strident, because orthodoxy's stance was the most complicated, both offensive (against Jewish claims to the Bible as well as against other Christian interpretations of it) and defensive (why claim the Book if they would not, in a sense, practice what they preached, and start living according to Jewish law?). But then why, by the fourth century, did imperial patronage not soften their tone? After all, by then this church had won. Its Christian competition was on the run; its communities were subsidized by government largesse; its bishops had powers that their secular counterparts (whose tenure in office was at most a few years; bishops, by contrast, held life appointments) could only envy. What was true in the second century was still true—save for the few bad moments in 362—in the fourth: the Jews had no temple and no territory. Why then, at this point, does the *contra Iudaeos* tradition only become worse—more strident, more comprehensive, more furious? It metastasizes through all known genres of surviving Christian literature, including systematic theologies, biblical commentaries, martyr stories, church histories, antiheretical tracts, preaching handbooks, sermons. Why?

It spread, I think, because of the Diaspora synagogue. Although we might expect that Jewish communities, now persecuted, should be shriveling up, the archaeological record states the opposite. Synagogues are thriving; in places like Sardis, they are monumental. Gentiles keep dropping by, cocelebrating Sabbaths and holidays, picking up the occasional Jewish practice, hearing Bible stories read and psalms sung in Greek (or, in the West, in Latin). Infuriatingly for the bishops, some of these Gentiles are not pagan (though some are), but Christian. The complaints in the sermons, the legislation—endlessly repeated—in the canons of contemporary church councils, give us a surprisingly vivid picture. Fourth-century Gentile Christians, despite the anti-Jewish ideology of their own bishops, kept Saturdays as their day of rest, accepted gifts of matzo from Jewish friends at Passover, indeed still celebrated Easter according to when the Jews kept Passover. This last was particularly aggravating to bishops, and even to emperors. Gentile Christians made the effort to take oaths in front of Torah scrolls, tended lamps for Jewish friends on the Sabbath and on Jewish holidays, had rabbis bless their fields, and let their children marry one another. Occasionally, and despite heavy penalties, these Christians even converted to Judaism. We can still hear the frustration and plaintive anger that this behavior inspired in a sermon, preached in August of 387 by the orthodox bishop of Antioch, John Chrysostom. Bracing for the imminent onslaught of the autumn high holidays—Rosh Hashanah, Yom Kippur, Sukkot—Chrysostom cried out to his synagogue-going congregation, "Don't you understand that if the Jews' way of life is true, then ours must be false?"

The anti-Judaism of the ideologues, the theologians and the bishops, increased in volume. Their pitch rose with their frustration. As long as Mediterranean social life was still intact, however, as long as the culture of the Hellenistic city with its long tradition of religious openness still lived—and it did live, well into the late Empire—Jews and Gentiles still mixed and mingled, saw each other at the baths and at the theaters, worked with each other on town councils, lived together, and, on Sabbaths and the holidays, occasionally heard Scripture together. When this changed, in the early Middle Ages, this tradition of civility changed too, and Christian anti-Judaism led more directly to violence, even murder. But this falls well outside the scope of my story.

How did Christian anti-Judaism happen? Gentiles interpreted the intra-Jewish disputes of the earliest Christian movement as the condemnation of all Judaism by those parties to the dispute with whom these Gentiles now identified. When did this happen? Toward the turn of the first century through the first half of the second, when warring Gentile Christian intellectuals staked out their territory and systematized their convictions into theologies. When, then, does Christianity begin? It is twice-born, once in the mid-second century, and again after Constantine, in the fourth. And in that second birth especially, orthodox Christian anti-Judaism increased in range and in intensity.

The answer to a fourth, and more important question, I leave to you: What, knowing this history, is today's Christian to do?

2

Jesus, Ancient Judaism, and Modern Christianity: The Quest Continues

E. P. Sanders

Discussing anti-Judaism and the historical Jesus is quite different from discussing anti-Judaism in (for example) the Gospel of Luke. The Gospel of Luke, unlike the historical Jesus, is a text that lies before us and that we can repeatedly study. The author wrote things about Jews, and those explicit statements can be analyzed in the context of the completed document. Jesus, however, left us no writings. We have, instead, diverse actions and sayings that are attributed to him in several Gospels. There are many minor disagreements among the Gospels, and occasionally major ones. These differences result from the fact that the material about Jesus was handed down from person to person and was put to use in various ways by early Christian teachers and evangelists. Moreover, the teaching of Jesus was translated from the Aramaic that he spoke into the Greek of the New Testament. The result is that a degree of uncertainty attaches to the material attributed to him. If we want to ask whether or not Jesus himself was an anti-Jewish Jew, we must first sift the material attributed to him and reconstruct his life and thought, while recognizing that all our decisions are somewhat tentative. The reconstructed Jesus, however, never becomes a text whose precise words can be studied and restudied.

Any historical reconstruction involves a subjective element. Thus we can also ask whether or not some scholars who have written about Jesus betray their own anti-Judaism. This is a slightly easier question to answer than are questions about Jesus, though it too involves some difficult issues, as we shall see.

In what follows, I shall assume that most of the material in the Synoptic Gospels (Matthew, Mark, and Luke) goes back to the historical Jesus, even when I have doubts about it. I do not wish to dismiss any criticisms of Judaism that might conceivably go back to the historical Jesus. I shall discuss scholarly opinions about Jesus by grouping them under large headings, giving as little detail about individual scholars' views as possible. Many New Testament scholars have been anti-Jewish, and some presumably still are. But the accusation is a serious one, and since in this chapter I cannot present a thorough study of an individual's writings, I wish not to specify and name people who have been or may be anti-Jewish.

THE HISTORICAL JESUS AND CHRISTIAN FAITH

I have already indicated that, since "the historical Jesus" must be recovered from disparate sources that sometimes disagree, each scholar has a good deal of choice about how to describe him. These choices, while doubtless including a subjective element, also rest on common academic views about how to ascertain the best evidence. New Testament scholars believe that not all the evidence is equally good, and thus they agree that there is a distinction between "the historical Jesus" and "Jesus as described in the Gospels." I believe that it will be helpful if I explain more fully the term "the historical Jesus" and say a few words about the relationship of the Jesus of history to Christian faith.

For almost a hundred years the phrase "the quest of the historical Jesus" has referred to the academic effort to recover Jesus of Nazareth, the man who lived in ancient Jewish Palestine ca. 4 B.C.E.–30 C.E. The quest itself is more than two hundred years old, and it continues today, constituting one of the main topics of New Testament research. Its basic assumption is that the Jesus of history became—or was turned into—the Christ of faith, the second person of the Trinity, as the result of theological development, but that an unadorned Jesus may be found behind or beneath early Christian literature.

Since the quest of the historical Jesus is recent and academic, we know that its results cannot be crucial to Christianity. The Christ of faith is, of course, crucial, but beliefs about him are not subject to historical investigation. Using the tools of historical investigation, we can study only the history of a belief (Paul thought X, John thought Y, Augustine thought Z, and so on), not its content. For example, that Christ sits at the right hand of the Father, that he is of the same essence as the Father, that he will return, and that God counts his death as a sacrifice that cancels the sins of those who believe in him are entirely matters of faith whose veracity can be neither affirmed nor denied by historical study. For the most part, Christianity rests on beliefs about God and Christ that cannot conceivably suffer at the rough hands of the historian.

On the other hand, Christianity does require *a* historical Jesus. Christians believe not only that Christ is of the same essence as the Father, but also that he is of the same essence as humans, "like us in all respects, apart from sin," as the Chalcedonian definition put it (451 C.E.). The church fathers regarded it as a heresy to deny that Jesus was fully human. Thus orthodox Christians have believed and still believe that there was a Jesus who was a living, breathing, suffering, and dying human being.

Christianity consequently requires *stories about* Jesus, such as those that are supplied by the Gospels. The stories, however, do not have to agree perfectly. The four Gospels present different images of Jesus. The conflicts and disagreements, which have always been recognized, usually do not trouble the believer. One Sunday, church members read and apply one story about Jesus, another Sunday another one, and so on. Christians require stories, but historical analysis, sifting, and reconstruction are optional extras. The historian notes that some of the stories in the Gospels are likelier than others and that some cannot be reconciled with others, which leads to the academic need to sort the evidence in order to reconstruct a believable picture of a single man who lived in ancient Jewish Palestine.

The quest of the historical Jesus is a requirement laid on us by our intellectual history, not by the needs of Christianity. Three great movements have largely shaped the modern Western world: the Renaissance (fourteenth–sixteenth centuries), the Protestant Reformation (sixteenth century), and the Enlightenment (seventeenth–eighteenth centuries). These movements contributed the critical study of ancient documents, including the exposure of errors, incongruities, and even forgery; a partial desacralization and demystification of Christianity; the view that the world follows rational principles and that human reason can conquer all. The historical and critical study of the Bible began in the seventeenth century (as a result of the Renaissance), but the quest of the historical Jesus did not arise until near the end of the Enlightenment period. The early questers were strongly influenced by a type of Enlightenment thought called "deism," which held that God created the world and established the natural laws that govern it, but thereafter did not interfere. Scholars influenced by deism thus dismissed the supernatural elements in the Gospels, such as miracles, or attributed them to natural causes. They sought a Jesus who was a great man rather than a semidivine being.

The desire to find a historical Jesus who was freed from the confines of Christian dogma and whose life did not constitute an irrational intrusion into the orderly world was very widespread in intellectual circles in the late eighteenth and early nineteenth centuries. Many of the early questers regarded dogma as outmoded and even as an obstacle to Christianity. In 1906, looking back on almost 130 years of scholarly efforts to find the historical Jesus, Albert Schweitzer wrote that academic research had loosed the bonds by which he had been riveted to "the stony rocks of ecclesiastical doctrine." For many Christians, the historical Jesus—a great and good man—emerged as a fresh and vital alternative to traditional institutional Christianity. The creeds were stuffy, ponderous, and so burdened with metaphysical issues that they obscured the living voice of the Man from Galilee. The historical Jesus would give them someone to follow—if only they could get to him.

Once the matter is put this way, it becomes clear that it is very tempting to describe a Jesus who is a suitable person to follow, someone who represents the *right* ideas and ideals. But, of course, people disagree about what these are. The result is that the selection of evidence often reflects the scholar's own estimate of what is worthy of emulation. What is common to all the questers, whether early or recent, is the view that some of the material in the Gospels is "authentic" and represents the real historical Jesus, who should be followed, while other material should be rejected. The reasons for rejection are diverse. Some passages are held to be based on later Christian dogma, while others are viewed as tainted with ancient superstitions (such as demon possession) and silly, pointless practices (such as purification).

Not infrequently, the parts of the Gospels that some people regard as silly and obviously bad, and which they wish not to attribute to Jesus, come from ancient Judaism. This gives an anti-Jewish bias to the separation of wheat from chaff. Arrival at this point means that we are now ready to come to grips with the issue of anti-Judaism and the historical Jesus. There are, as we noted above, two questions: Did Jesus himself oppose vital aspects of ancient Judaism? Are scholars who wish to distance him from ancient Judaism displaying their own anti-Judaism? We begin by emphasizing the first word in the phrase "ancient Judaism."

JESUS AS THE ONLY MODERN MAN
WHO LIVED IN THE ANCIENT WORLD

It is an odd fact, but many of the people whose interests take them into the study of the ancient world dislike it. In the case of many New Testament scholars, the only parts of the ancient world of which they have knowledge are those parts that crop up in the New Testament. In the study of Jesus, the ancient world that they encounter is Jewish. Since some of these scholars want to distance Jesus from his ancient environment, they often attack and denigrate Judaism, but in many cases what they actually dislike is the ancient world, and they simply attack the version of it that they meet in the Gospels. Their hearts, in other words, may be perfectly free of dislike of the Jewish people, and they might be perfectly happy with modern forms of Judaism that have discarded their ancient trappings. What they want is for Jesus to have been a modern man who spoke directly to modern concerns and who had sloughed off ancient superstitions and other mistaken views. We shall consider three aspects of ancient Judaism—ritual, exorcism, and apocalyptic eschatology—as illustrations of ancient views that are often disliked today.

Rituals

Rituals have been part and parcel of human life as far back as we can see, which is to the Stone Age. I shall not belabor this point; in order to see it, one need only think of ritual dancing by "primitive" peoples. Ritual continued to flourish in classical antiquity and in the Middle Ages. The three intellectual movements that shaped the modern Western world—the Renaissance, the Protestant Reformation, and the Enlightenment—all helped to demote ritual. The Protestants, for example, reduced the number of Christian sacraments from seven to two (baptism and the Lord's Supper, or Eucharist), which greatly diminished ritual in Protestant Christianity. Enlightenment thinkers, with their insistence on rationality, disliked ritual, which they saw as playing on emotions rather than appealing to rational thought. In the contemporary United States, of course, the "doctrine" of the separation of church and state has reduced ritual at the beginning of the school day and before football games by court rulings that exclude public prayer on these occasions. So ritual has a lot of enemies, and only a few ritual occasions survive. Graduation, marriage, and death are frequently accompanied by ritual ceremonies. Many people still salute the flag and stand when the national anthem is played, but outside of church and synagogue there are not many rituals, and in modern worship services there are fewer rituals than there were in the ancient, medieval, and early modern periods.

Despite this demotion, most of us are naturally drawn to ritual and solemn ceremonies when well performed. One of the reasons tourists go to Britain is to see well-executed ceremonies. The marriage of Prince Charles and Diana was watched by millions worldwide. Still, the ideologies that shaped the modern world dominate, and there is little ritual in the lives of most people. (Since this chapter was written, reactions to the tragedies of September 11, 2001, have revealed the recurrent human need for rituals. Partially new rituals were created, such as the lighting of a great mass of candles near the site of the World Trade Center.)

Since it is possible for people to perform rituals without directing their hearts and minds to what the ritual signifies, it is frequently suspected that those who perform rituals are hypocrites. This suspicion is old, going well back into the period of the Hebrew Bible (for example, Amos 5:21–24). Someone who is acting in an obviously pious manner is suspected of putting on a show, and the suspicion is very hard to counter. The more a religious person acts in accord with the precepts of her religion, the more she is suspected of hypocrisy.

The world in the time of Jesus was full of rituals—and, of course, some people suspected others of being hypocrites. *The rituals of ancient people who lived around the Mediterranean Sea were all approximately the same.* The commonest were sacrifice and purification. Throughout the ancient world, people sacrificed animals, and prepared themselves for these sacrifices by washing off impurities. They even agreed to a substantial degree on what made people impure. It was basically everything that was associated with the generation of life and its end, death. In many cultures, menstrual blood and corpses were believed to be sources of impurity. In Judaism, in addition to corpses and menstrual blood, semen, childbirth, and abnormal flows from the genitals (such as are caused by miscarriage and gonorrhea) resulted in impurity (Lev. 12, 15; Num. 19). "Leprosy" (not clinical leprosy, but one or more diseases that cause lesions, discoloration, or flaking of the skin; Lev. 13 and 14) does not conform to the usual type of impurity, since it is not part of the life cycle. Purification of leprosy and abnormal flows from the genitals required sacrifice as well as washing and waiting, while the other impurities required only washing and waiting. Some impurities required less waiting time (menstruation, semen), others more. Childbirth and contact with corpses—the beginning and end of life—required the longest waiting periods. After purification, one was free to enter the Temple, sacrifice, and share in the food produced by sacrifice. Various Jewish groups practiced other purifications besides those required for sacrifice. Some, for example, observed the extrabiblical custom of washing their hands before praying or before eating.

Many of these points about sacrifice and purity can be illustrated by passages written by two ancient Jews. The first is Philo of Alexandria, an older contemporary of Jesus, who was a pious, learned, and wealthy Jew. He frequently discussed paganism (or polytheism), and pointed out the superiority of Judaism. For example, he noted that polytheists, like Jews, symbolized purification by washing and sprinkling. Although the pagans purified themselves with water, he charged that

> they neither wish nor practise to wash off from their souls the passions by which life is defiled. They are zealous to go to the temples white-robed, attired in spotless raiment, but with a spotted heart they pass into the inmost sanctuary and are not ashamed. (Philo, *On the Cherubim*, 95f.)

Similarly, stated Philo, pagans would not sacrifice a blemished animal, but their own souls were full of wounds and sicknesses. When the Jews practiced ablutions, Philo maintained, they purified both body and soul. In his description of the rituals before entering the Temple in Jerusalem, he explains that those who "resort to the temple to take part in sacrifice must needs have their bodies made clean and bright, and before their bodies their souls" (*The Special Laws*, 1.269).

Philo had not actually managed to examine the soul of each pagan and each Jew who purified himself and sacrificed an animal. The charge of hypocrisy, such as he leveled against polytheists, is a useful rhetorical tool to employ when attacking someone with whom one disagrees. It is useful because it cannot be disproved: the accused person cannot demonstrate that her heart is aligned with her actions. People who are inclined to agree with the accuser can easily believe that the accused is a hypocrite.

The second writer, the anonymous author of the *Letter of Aristeas*, was an Egyptian Jew who lived about a hundred years earlier than Philo. According to the story of this work, the king of Egypt, Ptolemy, had decided to have the Hebrew Bible translated into Greek, and for this purpose had assembled seventy Jewish translators. Each day the translators washed their hands in the sea while praying to God. When asked why, "they explained that it was evidence that they had done no evil, for all activity takes place by means of the hands" (*Arist.*, 306). We do not know the origin of this practice. Possibly it was only reflection on such biblical passages as Psalm 24:4, which seems to equate "clean hands" and "pure hearts."

From these passages we learn three points:

1. Jews and pagans had very similar rituals, including especially sacrifice and purification.
2. It is easy to accuse people of hypocrisy who perform external actions—failing to align the inner person with the outer acts.
3. The acts themselves, however, were *intended* to assist the preparation of the heart or to illustrate that heart, mind, and body were in harmony with one another: pure hands point to pure intentions and pure deeds.

Some modern New Testament scholars think that Jesus opposed the Temple in Jerusalem, its sacrifices, or its priesthood (or some combination of these), and many more think that he opposed Jewish purity laws. In recent years, purity laws in particular have drawn the fire of scholars. Many of their views, to be sure, rest on ignorance about what Jewish purity laws actually were. Many scholars treat them as if they branded some people as bad, or as if they discriminated against women, ordinary people, the ill, or the poor. They sometimes write that impure people were considered "cut off" from the commonwealth of Israel.[1] In fact, most people were impure most of the time, and all were impure equally. Impurity was not a deficiency, nor did it make anyone an outcast. It had to be removed, however, before entering the Temple or eating sacrificial food.

All married adults frequently had semen-impurity; the vast majority of women had childbirth-impurity every two or three years, and every decent person contracted corpse-impurity when a friend or relative died. In Judaism, sexual intercourse, childbirth, and care for the dead were positive virtues. Menstruation, of course, was common to all females between puberty and menopause. Those impure from such causes had not sinned, nor did anyone find any sort of fault with them.

The point of the purity laws, both Jewish and non-Jewish, seems to have been to keep the chief insignia of human *change* out of the temple of the changeless deity. Thus most purity laws fix on either the genitals or death. We today do not have this concern. Consequently only a few people observe purity laws (some are still practiced in some forms of Judaism), and even fewer think that the signs of human generation and decay are offensive to God. Purity laws are distinctly nonmodern.

Animal sacrifice, which is equally nonmodern, is also offensive to many people today, since it seems a strange and brutal way to worship God. Thus purification, sacrifice, and more or less everything connected with them are looked down on today as deplorable, barbaric, ritualistic, externalistic, and the like. All the people who have such views dislike ancient religion; and, since religion permeated most aspects of life, they *dislike the ancient world*. Some of them, being unacquainted with other ancient religions, may regard themselves as critics of Judaism, but we cannot really consider them anti-Jewish. They are just anti-ancient.

What evidence do we have from the Gospels that supports the view that Jesus shared the modern dislike of purification and animal sacrifice? The passages that most directly deal with a purity law refer to skin disease ("leprosy"). According to Mark 1:40–45 (paralleled in Matt. 8:2-4 and Luke 5:12–16), Jesus *cleansed* a leper of his malady; that is, he *purified* him (since the same Greek word means both "cleanse" and "purify"). He then told him, "Show yourself to the priest, and offer for your cleansing [purification] what Moses commanded, as a testimony to them." According to this passage, Jesus—in accord with the ancient Jewish view—regarded the man's skin condition as an impurity (not an illness), since he "cleansed" or "purified" him, not "healed" him. He then ordered him to undergo the purification procedure required by the Mosaic law. The purification included the sacrifice of two birds plus one or more other animals, depending on the cleansed man's financial circumstances (Lev. 14:4, 10, 21–22). If this passage truly represents the historical Jesus, he believed in impurities, purifications, and sacrifice. There is a similar story in Luke 17:11–14. This time, Jesus cleanses ten lepers at once, telling them to show themselves to the priests.

The passage that most directly refers to sacrifice is Matt. 5:23–24, in which Jesus admonishes those who offer a "gift at the altar," that is, a sacrifice, first to be reconciled with anyone who has something against them. The sacrificial system, explicitly including the altar, is also accepted in Jesus' rebuke to the Pharisees for some of their views about which oaths are valid:

> How blind you are! For which is greater, the gift or the altar that makes the gift sacred? So whoever swears by the altar, swears by it and by everything on it; and whoever swears by the sanctuary, swears by it and by the one who dwells in it. (Matt. 23:19–21)

Besides pointing to Jesus' acceptance of sacrificial worship, this passage also indicates that he shared the view common in the ancient world that a temple was the house of a god. While the god or goddess might also be on Mount Olympus or in heaven, and was often thought of as omnipresent, he or she dwelt especially in the appropriate temple. Jews thought that the God of Israel dwelt especially in the Temple in Jerusalem, and that is precisely what made the space sacred and what necessitated purification rules. In Matthew 23:21 Jesus reflects the common Jewish view of the Temple as the dwelling place of God.

I shall very briefly mention a few other passages. In Mark 7:1–6 Jesus is presented as debating hand washing with "the Pharisees and some of the scribes." His disciples did not wash their hands before eating. Hand washing in Jesus' day was a growing custom among Jews. It is not mentioned in the Bible and was regarded by the Pharisees as a "tradition of the elders," not as part of the Jewish law—and, indeed, in Mark, Jesus criticizes them for observing this "tradition of the elders." Thus Jesus, like many, did not accept this Pharisaic practice, but this only shows that he was not a member of the very small Pharisaic party (no more than a few thousand), not that he rejected the biblical purity laws.

In Mark 5:25–34 (paralleled in Matt. 9:20–22 and Luke 8:43–48) there is a story of Jesus' healing a woman who had had a flow of blood for twelve years. This is an extreme case of an unnatural "discharge" from the genitals, which is an impurity (Lev. 15:25–30). The woman touched Jesus' garment and was healed. Jesus, conscious of being touched, turned and said to her that her faith had made her well. It is sometimes suggested that it was remarkable of Jesus to allow himself to be touched by an impure woman. But being touched by the impure was a daily or, in a city, an hourly fact of life. Streets were narrow and crowded, and more or less everyone was impure more or less all the time. Bumping into an impure person was not remarkable. More-over, the woman with a discharge of blood, like one who menstruates, con-veys impurity only to those who touch what she sits or lies on (Lev. 15:26–27). Touching in the street does not count.[2] What is more striking about the pas-sage is that the woman is regarded as being *ill* rather than *impure*, and thus she is healed (Mark 5:28, 34) rather than cleansed or purified. A discharge of blood for twelve years obviously indicated that something was seriously wrong; it was not a case of miscarriage or of irregular bleeding during preg-nancy. In any event, the passage tells us nothing about Jesus' views of purity and impurity.

Finally, we must consider a major event in the Gospels and doubtless in Jesus' life: his "cleansing" of the Temple (Mark 11:15–17; Matt. 21:12–13; Luke 19:45–46; John 2:14–16). The debates about the significance of this scene have been vigorous and wide-ranging. It appears at first to be a protest against dishonesty ("you have made it a den of robbers"). But a reference to the Temple's being a "house of prayer for all the nations" might indicate that Jesus objected to the exclusion of Gentiles from the inner court. Or, since other passages indicate that he either predicted or threatened the destruction of the Temple (for example, Mark 13:2; 14:58; 15:29), possibly what is called the "cleansing" (turning over tables in the Temple's forecourt) was actually a symbol of its coming destruction. These three main possibilities yield others: If he intended cleansing of dishonesty, did he object to the current chief priests, and would he have been content with a change of Temple officials? If he wanted the Temple to be a house of prayer for everyone, did he actually mean that he wanted the Temple to be a place of sacrifice for everyone, so that Gentiles as well as Jews would offer at God's altar? (During Jesus' lifetime and up until its destruction, the Temple *was* a "house of prayer for all nations"; the outermost court of the Temple precincts provided visiting pagans with just such space.) If he was symbolizing destruction, did he want to eliminate the Temple? Was he simply indicating where present political actions might lead? Did he expect the kingdom of God to arrive, in which case the Temple either would be superfluous or would be rebuilt?

Clearly we cannot answer all these questions. We can say, however, that this dramatic scene does not prove that Jesus was against Jewish sacrifices and purifications, particularly in light of other evidence in the Gospels. At the maximum, he objected to the policies of the present priestly leaders. Even if he was symbolically indicating the coming destruction of the Temple, we still would not know that he opposed animal sacrifice, since he might have expected its rebuilding or have been envisaging a transformed world in which sacrifice for sin would not be necessary. In any case, none of the sayings about the destruction of the Temple oppose sacrifice.

Scholars who propose that Jesus opposed the Temple as such (rather than its present administration) and/or the purity laws must either distort or ignore the evidence, according to which Jesus accepted purification and sacrifice. They must also ignore the *absence* of direct attacks on sacrifice, purification, tithing (which supported the Temple system), and the priesthood. Jesus attacks the Pharisees in Matthew 23, but the priests were the more powerful leaders. Why are there no attacks on them? It seems to me that if he had wanted to do away with the Jewish religion as such, which included, as all religions did, these very nonmodern elements, he might have said something about it, and his followers would presumably have passed on the information. But we find no evidence that he did.

To conclude this part of our discussion: There is some good evidence that Jesus accepted purification and sacrifice (as well as other ancient views, such as that God especially dwelt in the Temple), and there is no good evidence against it. Thus far we do not find Jesus to have been an anti-Jewish Jew. I am inclined to treat scholars who claim that he opposed *Judaism* because of its rituals and sacrifices as being only anti-ancient, not anti-Jewish.

Exorcism

The casting out of demons—exorcism—constitutes the largest category of miracle stories in the Synoptic Gospels. In summaries of Jesus' healing, Mark (for example) sometimes writes that Jesus "cast out many demons" and the like (1:34; see also 1:39). There are several specific stories of Jesus' exorcising demons (for example, Mark 7:24–30; Matt. 9:32–34; 17:14–18). Moreover, Jesus' followers could cast out demons (Mark 3:15; 6:13), as could some other Jews, such as the sons of the Pharisees (Matt. 12:27; Luke 11:19). Jesus' opponents did not doubt that he could cast out demons, they only suspected that he did so not by the power of God but by an alliance with the prince of demons (Mark 3:22). This reveals that Jesus' contemporaries did not doubt the existence of demons.

Other views of sickness and emotional illness have now replaced the theory of demonic possession. Although today some people would say that they believe in demons, few "really" believe in them, since few call in an exorcist when a loved one is ill or is behaving in an irrational and dangerous way. If anything, exorcism is even less popular in the modern world than is purification.

It takes a good deal of courage to say that Jesus was so much a part of his world that he believed in demons and their expulsion. Naturally, today people wish to "do something" with these stories, to get rid of them or interpret them so that Jesus' belief in demons, which connects him to an ancient world quite different from ours, is not so obvious. In sermons, "demons" can be interpreted as the doubts and fears that plague us all, and scholars readily (and possibly correctly) explain exorcism by the theory of psychosomatic cures (mind over body). Recently one scholar, John Dominic Crossan, has interpreted the story in Mark 5:1-13 as revealing a connection between demonic possession and Roman "colonial oppression," since the demon is named "Legion."[3] Here Crossan is careful to note that the story actually concerns the healing of an individual, but he wants to find its significance somewhere else. This reduces the offense to the modern mind.

Although frequently New Testament scholars regard impurity and purification as distinctively Jewish (though they are not), they generally recognize that belief in demons and in the power of exorcism were more widespread. Thus they do not criticize Judaism for such views. This topic deserves inclusion here because it helps to confirm the argument that many modern people would like to free Jesus of his ancient environment. The evidence of the healing stories, however, is that he shared it.

Apocalyptic Eschatology

This is the view that the end of the present order will be visually dramatic, accompanied by cosmic signs and figures descending from heaven. A good deal of apocalyptic eschatology is attributed to Jesus. The earliest passage is in 1 Thessalonians, which is the oldest surviving piece of Christian literature. There Paul attributes the following to "the word of the Lord" (1 Thess. 4:15):

> We who are alive, who are left until the appearance of the Lord, will by no means precede those who have died. For the Lord himself, with a cry of command, with the archangel's call, and with the sound of God's trumpet, will descend from heaven, and the dead in Christ will rise first. Then we who are alive, who are left, at the very same time will be caught up in the clouds together with them to meet the Lord in the air. (1 Thess. 4:15–17)

The study of 1 Thessalonians quickly reveals that the first sentence of this passage (v. 15) is Paul's addition. The problem in Thessalonica was that Paul had led his converts to expect the Lord to return in their lifetime, but that some had died. The surviving members of the church were concerned, fearing that the dead people would miss out on the new life in the kingdom of God, which would be established when Jesus returned. Paul replies by saying that the dead will in fact be raised to be with the Lord first. The rest of the saying, verses 16–17, which describes the Lord's descent from heaven, is very close to numerous passages about the Son of Man that are attributed to Jesus in the Synoptic

Gospels. To demonstrate this, compare the passage in 1 Thessalonians side by side with two passages from Matthew. The closest similarities are indicated by italics.

---

1 Thessalonians Compared with Mattthew's Version of Passages 1 and 2 Below

1 Thessalonians 4:15–17	Matthew 24:30–31	Matthew 16:27–28
We who are alive, who are left until the *coming of the Lord*, will by no means precede those who have died. For *the Lord* himself, with a cry of command, with the *archangel's* call and *with the sound of God's trumpet*, will *descend* from *heaven*, and the dead in Christ will rise first. Then *we who are alive* . . . will be *caught up* together in the clouds with them to meet the Lord in the air.	The sign of the *Son of Man will appear* in heaven, and then all the tribes of earth will mourn, and they will see 'the *Son of Man coming* on the clouds of *heaven*' with power and great glory. And he will send out his *angels with a loud trumpet call*, and they will *gather* his elect from the four winds, from one end of heaven to the other.	*The Son of Man* is to *come* with his *angels* in the glory of his Father, and then he will repay everyone for what has been done. Truly I tell you, there are some standing here who *will not taste death* before they see the Son of Man coming in his kingdom.

Comparison of these passages indicates that Paul thought that Jesus referred to himself when he spoke of the coming of "the Son of Man," and thus Paul writes of the appearance of "the Lord" (Jesus) rather than of "the Son of Man." The question of what Jesus thought about his own relationship to this heavenly figure has been much debated, without yielding a thoroughly satisfactory result.

The tradition common to Paul and Matthew constitutes only a fraction of the evidence for apocalyptic eschatology in the teaching of Jesus. The principal passages are as follows:

1. Cosmic distress, Son of Man, angels, gather elect: Matthew 24:29–31; Mark 13:24–27; Luke 21:25–28. (Part of the passage in Matthew is quoted above)
2. Son of Man, glory of Father, angels, some present will not taste death: Matthew 16:27–28; Mark 8:38–9:1; Luke 9:26–27. (The Matthean passage is quoted above)
3. The day of the Son of Man, lightning, Noah: Matthew 24:27, 37–39; Luke 17:24, 26, 27, 30.
4. Jesus' trial: the Son of Man seated at the right hand of power, coming on clouds: Matthew 26:64; Mark 14:62; Luke 22:69.

Of all the material in the Gospels that modern scholars wish would disappear, this probably ranks first. And, in fact, it does disappear in many of their books. But as we have just seen, the expectation of a heavenly figure descending is extremely well supported in ancient Christian texts. It is one of the best-supported traditions, more or less equal to the prohibition of divorce. In terms of source analysis, one finds it in Paul, in the Markan tradition (that is, among passages that are common to all three Synoptic Gospels), and in the Q tradition (that is, among passages that are common to Matthew and Luke but absent from Mark). These are usually regarded as three independent traditions, and it appears in more than one version in the Markan material. Such evidence as this ordinarily convinces scholars that a passage is "authentic."

The idea that Jesus had such views is, of course, difficult for some modern Christians to accept. Moreover, if he held the opinion that Paul, Matthew 16:28, and Mark 9:1 attribute to him (some of the present generation will still be alive), he was seriously in error, since all the people alive at that time have now been dead for quite a while, and the heavenly figure has still not arrived. Naturally many people, in the academy as well as in the church, wish to prevent Jesus from making an error, even one of timing; and so apocalyptic eschatology is an aspect of Judaism that many New Testament scholars would like to see eliminated from Christianity.

Here again we see the desire to separate Jesus from an ancient Jewish idea now regarded with distaste. To indulge this preference in effect cuts Jesus out of his historical and religious context, but does fit him nicely into ours. Such a desire does not mean that these scholars are anti-Jewish, nor that they are opposed to Judaism and Jews as such. It means, rather, that they are uncomfortable with an aspect of Jesus' message that conformed to one ancient Jewish view.

JUDAISM: WRATH AND WORKS

Two of the most common and most erroneous views about Judaism held by Christians are, first, that Judaism was a religion of wrath, punishment, and divine vengeance, whereas Christianity introduced love, mercy, and grace; and, second, that Judaism was a religion that emphasized human works rather than divine grace. We shall consider these in turn.

Wrath versus Mercy

A biblical passage seems to support the view that Judaism teaches "wrath" while Christianity teaches "mercy": "The law indeed was given through

Moses; grace and truth came through Jesus Christ" (John 1:17). This verse does not precisely say that the law teaches only wrath and that Judaism lacked the idea of mercy, though Christians frequently read it in the light of this conviction. In its simplest form, the contrast of a God of merciless vengeance with a God of compassion is more prevalent among Christian laypeople than among scholars. Almost everyone who goes to church knows Matthew 5:38–42:

> You have heard that it was said, "An eye for an eye and a tooth for a tooth." But I say to you, Do not resist an evildoer. . . .

The law of retaliation (Exod. 21:23-24) has often been quoted to me as giving the essence of Judaism, though in its original context it aimed only at eliminating a spiral of escalating individual retaliation (the person who loses a tooth knocks out two, the person who loses two teeth knocks out four, and so on). Similarly the sentence "He [the Lord] said: . . . Vengeance is mine, and recompense" (Deut. 32:20, 35) is intended to abolish private vengeance in favor of reliance on divine justice; Paul quotes the sentence in this sense (Rom. 12:19).

Somewhat more to the point, there are parts of the Hebrew Bible, especially the book of Joshua, that attribute to God some really vicious statements, including the admonition to eliminate every resident of a territory that the Israelites were conquering (for example, Josh. 10:8; 11:14–15). Joshua, in fact, is about as bloodthirsty as the book of Revelation in the New Testament (see Rev. 8:4–6; 9:18; 14:9-11; 19:17–21; 21:8). Lots of people like to envisage the destruction of their enemies. Those who prove cases by selective reading can thus "establish" that Jews (and Christians!) relished the idea of the destruction of their enemies.

A Christian who was accused of believing in a bloodthirsty God (on the basis of Revelation) would answer: Read the rest of the New Testament. That is approximately what we should say in answer to the assertion that the God of Judaism is concerned entirely with wrath and punishment. If anyone takes into account the whole of the Hebrew Bible and the views of Jews in Jesus' own day, the result is quite different. God is consistently regarded as a God of mercy, ever ready to forgive sinners. Moreover the God of the Israelites commands that his people love others, including even their enemies:

> You shall not take vengeance or bear a grudge against any of your people, but you shall love your neighbor as yourself: I am the LORD. (Lev. 19:18)

> The alien who resides with you shall be to you as the citizen among you; you shall love the alien as yourself, for you were aliens in the land of Egypt: I am the LORD your God. (Lev. 19:34)

> If your enemies are hungry, give them bread to eat; and if they are thirsty, give them water to drink. (Prov. 25:21)

> Do not say, "I will repay evil." (Prov. 20:22)

Postbiblical Jewish literature frequently emphasizes the same themes:

> We are men who worship God, and it does not befit a man who worships God to repay evil for evil nor to trample underfoot a fallen (man) nor to oppress his enemy till death. (*Joseph and Aseneth* 29.3-4)

> We [Jews] must . . . show consideration even to declared enemies. He [Moses] does not allow us to burn up their country or to cut down their fruit trees, and forbids even the spoiling of fallen combatants; he has taken measures to prevent outrage to prisoners of war, especially women. (Josephus, *Against Apion* 2.212)

> Do not do to anyone what you would not wish to be done to you. (Tobit 4:15; Philo, *Hypothetica* 7.6; Hillel in the Babylonian Talmud, *Shabbat* 31a)

Laypeople may be excused for not knowing all this. Moreover, they know a New Testament passage that seems to support the stark contrast between "wrath" (Judaism) and "love" (Christianity):

> You have heard that it was said, "You shall love your neighbor and hate your enemy." But I say to you, Love your enemies and pray for those who persecute you. (Matt. 5:43–44)

This passage quotes Leviticus 19:18, "Love your neighbor as yourself," and then it adds the reverse, "Hate your enemy." The second half is not a quotation from the Bible, though doubtless there were some Jews who hated their enemies (as some Christians hate theirs). If one takes "Hate your enemy" as representing all of Judaism, as some do, the contrast between "Christianity" and "Judaism" is denigrating to Judaism, since it is not true that Judaism taught hatred of enemies. Some Christian scholars have dealt with this passage responsibly. Christians who want to be fair to Judaism while also emphasizing the very high ethics attributed to Jesus in the Sermon on the Mount could say, with W. D. Davies and Dale Allison,

> Despite all the [Jewish] parallels just listed, the succinct, arresting imperative, "Love your enemies," is undoubtedly the invention of Jesus' own mind, and it stands out as fresh and unforgettable.[4]

I think that this is the better way of putting the matter: succinct, arresting, fresh, and unforgettable.

Sometimes a scholar who knows better nevertheless uses this one verse in Matthew as proving the superiority of Christianity to Judaism. This may very well qualify as "anti-Judaism." Even so, however, the actual motive may be simply the desire to depict Christianity as *morally superior* to Judaism. This requires further consideration.

Most people want to believe that their way of life is best, and in fact the best ever: "My religion is the only true one, my nation is the greatest the world has ever seen." A historian of Islam, Mohamed Amin, wrote this about the experience of pilgrimage to the sacred cities of Islam:

> To the pilgrim, the Mosque in Medina is alive with faith and everything in which a Muslim believes, for here was where the virtues of goodness, brotherhood, unselfishness and love first blossomed.[5]

Since Jesus lived some centuries before Muhammad, Christians will doubt that goodness and love *first* blossomed at the Mosque in Medina. And since Deuteronomy and Leviticus preceded Jesus by some centuries, Jews will doubt that Jesus brought love into the world. To evaluate Amin's statement more precisely, however, we should emphasize the first words: "*To the pilgrim*" love originates at Medina. He is not making the claim that in fact love began there, but rather that this is its source in the lives of faithful Muslims. Similarly, to Christians, it is Jesus who teaches love of neighbor. They learn it from him. In her Christmas message in 1989, Her Majesty Queen Elizabeth II urged her hearers to live by the rule "which Jesus Christ taught us, 'Love thy neighbour as thyself.'" I do not doubt that the head of the Church of England learned this from the teaching of Jesus, nor do I fault her for saying so. Few of the people in an average church pew will know that Jesus quoted Leviticus. Whether they know the Jewish background or not, it remains true that they learn it from Jesus. They may not live up to it, any more than Muslims manage to show love in all cases, but at least they have it as an ideal, and it comes to them from Jesus, no matter who may actually have said it first.

Staying with the question of chronological priority for one more moment, I should say something about the actual origin of love in each of our lives. The vast majority of people in the history of humanity have imbibed love with their mother's milk. Concretely, we learn love and mercy from our parents. Attributing Love to God absolutizes it and raises it from the level of our common humanity to a major principle, taught from heaven, by which we should guide our lives. But none of the historical religions actually created the idea that humans are loved by a higher power and that they should respond by loving that power and one another. That is the common inheritance of Judaism, Christianity, and Islam from the much longer history of humanity.

I am arguing that Christian confessions of faith (grace and truth came into *the world*—that is, to *our world*, to *us believers*—through Jesus) are not, in and of themselves, anti-Jewish. It is anti-Jewish, however, when people who make this confession then try to eliminate love and grace from the teaching of Judaism. Such efforts are historically incorrect and result in the denigration of Judaism. Christianity is different from Judaism because it is based on faith that the saving power of God was made manifest in Jesus, not because it teaches superior ethical principles for the guidance of our lives. Christianity inherited ethical and moral standards from Judaism, and Christians should thank Christianity's parent for them, rather than claiming that the parent lacked them.

Legalism

We now turn to the Christian view that Judaism was a religion of works and thus was "legalistic." This may be the most common item on Christian lists of the supposed faults of Judaism. The words "legalism" and "legalistic" in Christian usage mean more than that Judaism is based on divine law. They mean, rather, that Jews believe that they are *saved* by obeying the law rather than by faith in God and that they have *rejected* the idea that God saves because he is merciful. They hold, rather, that he saves only those who *save themselves* by doing more works of the law than the number of their transgressions.

The following is a list of the elements of legalism as I have inferred them from decades of reading Christian scholars who criticize ancient Judaism—and, by implication, modern Judaism.

1. In legalism, a person stands alone before God, with the obligation of doing enough good deeds to earn God's favor. There is no prior grace, there are no group benefits.
2. Salvation is attained by doing more good deeds than bad deeds.
3. Legalists believe that God is basically an accountant, a judge who is inflexibly controlled by human performance and who is occupied in keeping score. This divine accountant sends people with 51 percent good deeds to eternal bliss, people with 49 percent good deeds to eternal damnation.
4. Legalists have, then, a natural inclination to pile up a lot of easy good deeds. This leads to the pursuit of trivial acts of piety, such as tithing mint, dill, and cummin.
5. Trivial acts of piety lead to hypocrisy: showing off minor external actions while ignoring the most important religious principles.
6. Psychologically, the legalist is either *anxious* because he or she does not know whether or not enough good deeds have been compiled, or *arro-*

gant because of having done so many trivial good deeds that God will be forced to save her or him. There is no happy confidence in God because of God's love and mercy, since the legalist's God lacks these qualities.

7. The legalist believes in repentance in a very deficient way. Each act of repentance offsets one bad deed: that is, repentance is only one more meritorious work.

8. Within legalism, only one factor offers relief from strict judgment in accord with the number of good and bad deeds: a treasury of merits based on works of supererogation. Saintly legalists have more good deeds than they need, and God will apply some of these to offset the deficiencies of others. In particular, these supererogatory deeds may tip the scale in favor of people who have precisely 50 percent good and 50 percent evil deeds.

When Christians say that Judaism is a legalistic religion, they are saying that, from the point of view of the subject—the religious person—being a legalist is absolutely terrible (it leads to anxiety or arrogance), and moreover that legalism induces bad behavior (triviality and hypocrisy).

Hundreds, possibly thousands of New Testament scholars have charged Jews with being legalistic, and they have attributed to Jesus the desire to overcome the legalism of his native religion. I do not know all the reasons that led to this charge, but a partial explanation is this: In the eighteenth and nineteenth centuries, especially through the influence of the Enlightenment, Christian confidence in the creeds began to fail. Christians (we noted above) are supposed to believe that Jesus is 100 percent divine and 100 percent human. The Chalcedonian definition of 451 C.E. further specifies that the two natures in him were neither mixed, confused, nor separated. Christians could have carried on attacking Jews for not believing this, or for not accepting a Tri-une God, but these creedal formulations became less significant within liberal Protestantism, in which humanism came more and more to the fore. Christians who lost confidence in the creeds were still Christians, and they believed that their religion was superior to all others. But now they needed to prove it on humanistic, not theological or dogmatic grounds. In particular, Christians needed to prove that Christianity was superior to Judaism. Otherwise, why would it exist at all? Surely Jesus and Paul saw something basically and intrinsically wrong in Judaism, or there would be no new religion. In the age of liberal humanism, in which humanity is the measure of all things, Judaism must be proved to produce bad human beings.

The charge of legalism perfectly fitted the Christian need to accuse Judaism of producing bad humans. Legalistic Jews are either anxious or arrogant; they value trivial external actions; they are hypocrites. But now we must come to the question of evidence: What material did New Testament scholars cite as proving that Judaism was legalistic? In part they relied on New Testament passages, such as Matthew 23 and Matthew 6. I quote a few verses from these chapters:

Then Jesus said to the crowds and to his disciples, "The scribes and the Pharisees sit on Moses' seat; therefore, do whatever they teach you and follow it; but do not do as they do, for they do not practice what they teach. . . . They do all their deeds to be seen by others; for they make their phylacteries broad and their fringes long. They love to have the place of honor at banquets and the best seats in the synagogues, and to be greeted with respect in the marketplaces, and to have people call them rabbi." (Matt. 23:1–3, 5–7)

"Woe to you, scribes and Pharisees, hypocrites! For you tithe mint, dill, and cummin, and have neglected the weightier matters of the law: justice and mercy and faith. It is these you ought to have practiced without neglecting the others." (Matt. 23:23)

"So whenever you give alms, do not sound a trumpet before you, as the hypocrites do in the synagogues and in the streets, so that they may be praised by others. Truly I tell you, they have received their reward. . . . And whenever you pray, do not be like the hypocrites; for they love to stand and pray in the synagogues and at the street corners, so that they may be seen by others." (Matt. 6:2, 5)

Here we find many of the ingredients of legalism: emphasis on trivial, external actions, together with the accusations that the Jewish leaders in question act in these ways from bad motives (to be seen by other people), that their lives do not square with what they profess (they are hypocrites), and that they ignore the important values of justice, mercy, and faith. The passages, however, actually criticize only some people within Judaism, not all Jews, nor Judaism itself. New Testament scholars, of course, generalized these faults so that they became typical of Judaism. In the hands of the critics of Judaism, the Jewish attachment to Jewish law (the Torah) necessarily leads to legalism, which becomes a *system* that *makes* people act in these deplorable ways.

How should we reply to the accusation that Judaism is legalistic? I would urge that we consider four points. The first is a reminder that religious polemic (verbal attack) frequently focuses on motives and frequently charges that external actions and internal spirit do not coincide. It can do so because motives and internality are invisible. Philo, as we have seen, accused pagans of purifying their bodies and not their hearts or souls. He charged that they never really repented. There were in fact pagan saints, people whose hearts were unblemished, and who used the symbolic rituals of pagan religion to purify themselves entirely, both within and without. Philo says not, but this is merely cheap polemic. I am even surer that most of the Jews who gave alms or who prayed where they could be seen had the highest and purest motives. Vanity is, to be sure, a human and religious failing, and it afflicts a lot of people. But one can be vain about secret donations, and one need not be vain about public donations. This is true in the modern world, and so, we should think, of ancient Jews. Many of the charges of legalism against ancient Jews depend on cheap rhetoric about supposed failings within.

Second, we should recall Paul's ferocious attacks on other Christian leaders and apostles, including Peter. In Galatians he claims that Peter acted hypocritically when he first ate with Gentiles and then withdrew to eat only with Jews (Gal. 2:11–14). I would suggest that perhaps Peter had the highest motives, and that he came to fear that his mission to Jews might be compromised if he associated too closely with former idolaters. Paul said of himself that he was all things to all people in order to win some; that with Jews he lived as under the law, with Gentiles as not under the law (1 Cor. 9:19-23). This is not hypocrisy, but diplomacy. Should we accuse Paul of hypocrisy anyway? I think not—nor should Paul have accused Peter of acting hypocritically. Let us grant that ancient religious leaders, whether Jewish or Gentile, whether Christian or not, whether Pauline or not, on the whole acted from good motives. The charge that Jews did not do so is a worthless and base accusation. Jews were highly conscious of the need for right intention.

Third, we should reconsider the frequent contrast between Grace and Works, and the claim that Christianity is a religion of grace and Judaism is a religion of works, which is basic to the list of eight points above. The truth is that Jews, just like Christians, believed both that God, who was gracious, would save them by his mercy *and* that he required upright behavior and forbade evil deeds. This view can be proved by literally hundreds of pages of Jewish literature—which I refrain from quoting. But consider this: to this day, when Jews or Christians pray to God, they thank him for his numerous acts of mercy and for giving them the strength and ability to live as they should. They also recognize that in comparison to God, humans are weak creatures who must rely on divine strength and goodness. Yet when these same people falter, they do not blame God, they blame themselves. They seek to return to the path of righteousness, and they know that they must exert effort to do so. That is to say, humans are dependent on grace and they are accountable for their deeds. This is a common and, as far as I know, the universal view in both Judaism and Christianity, and it is puzzling that many Christian scholars who accept both aspects of religion in their own lives believe that in the ancient world these were mutually exclusive alternatives. They hold that since ancient Jews believed in upright behavior and observed the law they must have rejected grace! Reliance on grace and responsibility to perform suitable works are actually two sides of the same coin. They are simply different perspectives that arise in slightly different circumstances. One set of thoughts arises in prayer or meditation, the other in considering the practicalities and difficulties of daily life. The two can combine in one sentence, as in this passage from the Qumran Hymns: "No one can be righteous in your judgment or [inno-cent] in your trial, though one person may be more righteous than another" (1QH 9:14f.).

The fourth and final observation about the charge of legalism is funda-mental: no one in the ancient world was a legalist. Legalism, in the full Protes-tant meaning of the word, did not exist; it is a *modern invention*. The Jewish conception was (and still is) that the Jewish people were chosen by God prior to observance of the law, and that Jews are born into the covenant that God established by his grace. Converts to Judaism enter a preexistent covenant based on grace. Christian New Testament scholars who accuse Judaism of legalism must imagine that, in the Jewish view, each individual had to stand on his or her own merits, and that each had to earn God's grace. But no ancient Jew, and probably no ancient person, thought this *individualistically*. Individu-alism has been growing, by fits and starts, for at least three thousand years, but once upon a time all people thought of themselves first of all as members of a group. Jews to this day have a firmer consciousness of group solidarity than do most other people in the West.

There is a mass of evidence to show that in Jesus' day Jews believed that God had shown them grace before laying requirements on them. Here I can only illustrate the point. First of all, the idea of prior grace is intrinsic to the biblical story of Israel. Abraham was chosen before he was given command-ments. The people of Israel were brought out of Egypt before God gave the law at Mount Sinai. They did not earn the exodus by meritorious behavior. The Rabbis were well aware of this fact. I quote from *Mekhilta* Bahodesh 5 (the early rabbinic commentary on Exodus):

> Why were the Ten Commandments not said at the beginning of the Torah? They give a parable. To what may this be compared? To the following: A king who entered a province said to the people: May I be your king? But the people said to him: Have you done anything good for us that you should rule over us? What did he do then? He built the city wall for them, he brought in the water supply for them, and he fought their battles. Then he said to them: May I be your king? They said to him: Yes, yes. Likewise, God. He brought the Israelites out of Egypt, divided the sea for them, sent down the manna for them, brought up the well for them, brought the quails for them. He fought for them the battle with Amalek. Then he said to them: I am to be your king. And they said to him: Yes, yes.

And then, of course, God gave the Ten Commandments and the rest of the Mosaic law. The requirement of obedience in Judaism is and has always been second, after the call and redemption of the people.[6]

There are lots of rabbinic statements to the effect that God punishes transgression and rewards obedience.[7] Do these statements prove that a lot of good deeds would earn salvation, while a lot of bad deeds would earn damnation? That is not the point of the passages. It is, rather, that God is just and fair rather than capricious. Would you have him do the reverse—reward iniquity and punish good behavior? Of course not.

The importance of grasping the larger context of a religion can be seen very clearly if we look at the New Testament. Christians frequently read or hear read the following passage:

> For if you forgive others their trespasses, your heavenly Father will also forgive you; but if you do not forgive others neither will your Father forgive your trespasses. (Matt. 6:14–15)

This could be taken to mean that Christians have to *earn* forgiveness by *first* forgiving. But, of course, Christians think that God acted in Jesus' death to provide forgiveness. The sentence should not be lifted out of that context. One could conceivably prove that an individual author, such as Matthew, was a legalist, but such a conclusion could not prove that Christianity is a religion of legalism.

That is, in reading the New Testament, Christian scholars take context into account. In condemning Judaism as legalistic, they exclude context and focus on a few sentences. But in Judaism, as in Christianity, reward and punishment fall within the larger and more fundamental context of God's love.

The Christian charge against Judaism has been that Judaism as such is legalistic and that it *forces* its members into legalism. Here we can be decisive. Hypocrisy existed in the ancient world, as did impure motives and religious deceit, but this is all part of the human condition and is not specific to (much less systematically expressed and endorsed by) one culture. Historically, the charge of legalism is not true, and eliminating it from the arsenal of New Testament scholars who think that in order to make Christianity look good they must besmirch Judaism, would do the world a lot of good. If New Testament scholars were to drop this charge, and say explicitly that they drop it, perhaps clergy would give it up as well. Through them, perhaps the laity would come to a fairer assessment of Judaism. This, it seems to me, is a reasonable and achievable goal. In fact, fairness requires that we strive to reach it.

Let me say one last word on context. Christian commentators on Judaism in effect insert the question, "What must I do to be saved?" when they discuss Jewish, and especially rabbinic comments about the importance of observing the law. Then they conclude that the view that the law should be obeyed is an answer to the question, "How can I be saved?" But that is not a question that is large in Jewish literature in general, and it is minute in rabbinic literature. One can turn hundreds of pages of ancient Jewish literature, including especially rabbinic literature, without finding this question. Jews knew what they had to do to be saved. They had to rely on God, who called Abraham and made promises to him. Of course, the promises were based on the assumption that he and his descendants would be more or less obedient. But no Jew thought that he or she started with a blank slate and that he or she must fill it with good deeds in order to be saved. Jews started as members of the covenant, which was established by God's grace. They held that God was faithful never to break the covenant, as Paul himself says in Romans 11:29. Obedience was the natural response to the God who called Abraham and who brought Israel out of bondage.

CONCLUSION

There is no good evidence that Jesus was an anti-Jewish Jew. He did not reject worship by sacrifice, which was a central institution of Judaism (as of ancient religion in general), nor the practices required by it, such as purification and support of the Temple and the priesthood. Some of the scholars who think that Jesus opposed ritual, purification, and sacrifice believe that they are thereby setting him against Judaism, whereas in fact they are proposing that he was a modern man who only incidentally lived in the ancient world. The motive, I have suggested, is not anti-Judaism, but the desire to make Jesus and his message immediately relevant to contemporary society. The evidence from the Gospels, however, indicates that Jesus accepted the Jewish version of ancient religion, as well as the common belief that illness and mental problems were often caused by demonic possession.

He probably did criticize and argue with some of his contemporaries, but the criticisms that we find in the Gospels are rather modest in comparison to the words that some of the biblical prophets, such as Amos and Hosea, directed against their contemporaries. Moreover, criticisms of *some* people show approval of the larger society or of the religious and social system. The critic charges that some people are not living up to the right standard, with the implication that they are able to do so. The effort to improve a group shows that one affirms the group. We all feel quite free to criticize the leaders of our government, but this does not mean that we are opposed to our nation; on the contrary, we just want it to be better, and our criticisms are often the best evidence of our loyalty.

Genuine anti-Judaism, however, has been a feature of many scholarly descriptions of Jesus. Both laypeople and (with much less excuse) New Testament scholars have defined Jesus as the moral and religious opposite of his Jewish contemporaries. In arguing this case they have made statements that are denigrating to Judaism and that are historically false. It is not true that Judaism was legalistic. It is not true that Judaism was a religion of wrath and vengeance, which rejected love and mercy. It is not true that Jesus opposed the essentials of Judaism. His arguments with and criticisms of fellow Jews all stand within the wide boundaries of intra-Jewish discussion and debate. They measure not rejection, but commitment. Jesus lived, worked, and taught *within* first-century Jewish society and culture. If we now seek him, whether as clergy or as laypeople or as historians, then that is where we too must look.

NOTES

1. For example, N. T. Wright, *Jesus and the Victory of God* (Minneapolis: Fortress Press, 1996), p. 192.
2. Wright incorrectly states that the woman rendered anyone or anything that she touched impure; see *Jesus and the Victory of God*, p. 192.
3. J. Dominic Crossan, *Jesus: A Revolutionary Biography* (San Francisco: Harper-Collins, 1994), pp. 88–91.
4. W. D. Davies and Dale C. Allison Jr., *The Gospel according to Saint Matthew*, International Critical Commentary, vol. 1 (Edinburgh: T. &. T. Clark, 1988), p. 552.
5. Mohamed Amin, *Pilgrimage to Mecca* (London: Alan Hutchison, 1978), p. 28.
6. Many Jews dislike descriptions of Judaism that contain terms like "prior grace," because they regard the terminology as Christian. The terms, however, fit ancient Jews' conceptions of their relationship with God perfectly well.
7. E. P. Sanders, *Paul and Palestinian Judaism* (Philadelphia: Fortress Press, 1977), pp. 117–28.

3

Paul, the Apostle of Judaism

John Gager

On May 6, 2001, television stations around the world featured Pope John Paul II's visit to Christian sites in Syria. He wanted, so the media dutifully reported, to retrace the steps of the apostle Paul on the road to Damascus (the modern capital of Syria), where "he was converted to Christianity." At the same time, a certain confusion crept into these reports, for Paul was often cited as the real founder of Christianity. It is difficult to imagine how he could have been converted to Christianity while at the same time serving as its founder!

It may seem odd to begin the study of Paul, an ancient figure, by looking at confused images of him from later centuries. But we have good reasons for beginning in the present whenever we seek to understand the past. It is a truism that we can never approach the past directly. This is especially so for Christianity, where so much history and controversy stand between us and the origins of the Christian movement in the first and second centuries. We are always separated from the past by many intervening factors—time, language, culture, and even religion. The problem is not simply that the beliefs, experiences, and conditions of the past may (and usually do) differ greatly from our own, but even more seriously that our knowledge of the past is shaped by so many intervening images. By examining these images, we may be able to see through them to a less-obstructed view of Paul in his own time and place.

But we should not deceive ourselves. It will never be possible to meet the "real" Paul. We will always approach him (or any other figure of the past) through images and impressions—some from his friends, some from his enemies, and some, of course, from Paul himself. My argument will be that conflicting images of the apostle had already emerged in his own lifetime. He himself was well aware of these contradictory views. At various points he complains of being misunderstood by his own followers (see 1 Cor. 5:9–13; 6:12–20; Gal. 1:6–17; 5:11–12). He saw some of these views of himself and of his mission as total distortions, and in his letters he sought to "correct" them. But he failed. In the end, the dominant images that have come down to us are of a "domesticated apostle,"[1] a figure whose "argument has been reversed into the opposite to his original intention."[2]

Of all the images that we have inherited (Paul the misogynist, Paul the irascible egotist, Paul the systematic theologian, among others), the one I wish to focus on here is that of Paul as the father of Christian anti-Judaism, the author of rejection-replacement theology, who claimed that God has rejected his people Israel and replaced them with a new people, the Christians. According to this image, Paul converted from Judaism and became the second founder of Christianity. In the process he negated the religion of Jesus and repudiated Judaism entirely. The main elements in this picture are drawn from Paul's letters:

> His chief goal as a young Jew was to live according to the law of Moses, the Torah (Phil. 3:5).
>
> He adopted a harshly critical stance toward violators of the law, among them the early followers of Jesus (Phil. 3:6).
>
> He found himself unable to uphold the law and blamed his failure on his lower, carnal nature. In the end, he realized that the law itself was at fault, for it led inevitably to sin and transgression (Rom. 7:5–8).
>
> In Jesus, he encountered the solution to his tormented dilemma. Jesus had revealed the law to be false and destructive, and offered a new path to salvation (Rom 7:24–25).

From the very beginning Paul was the subject of intense controversy and debate. Virtually every type of Christianity sought to claim his authority for their version of the new faith. This was so much so that Tertullian, a major Christian writer of the late second century and a staunch defender of emerging orthodox Christianity, characterized Paul as the "apostle of heretics [*haereticorum apostolus*]" (*Against Marcion* 3.5.10). Of course, Tertullian did not mean to suggest that Paul was himself a heretic. His point was that the apostle had been commandeered by various Christian groups—above all by Marcion and by a series of Christian gnostics—whom Tertullian and others regarded as heretics. From Tertullian's perspective, these perverse heretics had distorted Paul's views to suit their own beliefs and practices. But such "misappropriations" were nothing new in Tertullian's time. Somewhat earlier in the second century, the New Testament writing known as 2 Peter lamented the use of Paul by unnamed Christian false teachers:

> Our beloved brother Paul wrote to you . . . , speaking of this as he does
> in all his letters. There are some things in them hard to understand,
> which the ignorant and unstable twist to their own destruction, as they
> do the other scriptures. (2 Pet. 3:15–16)

Here is the lesson: *From the very beginning, Paul's teachings, and his letters, were
subject to wildly divergent interpretations. Even in his own lifetime he was the focus
of major controversy.*

Not everyone loved Paul. During the second century, he became the target of intense hatred from various groups designated by historians as Jewish Christians—groups who continued to observe the laws of Moses
(circumcision, kosher foods, etc.) while worshiping the figure of Jesus. For
them, Paul was the archenemy since, in their view, he had repudiated the
Torah, not just for Gentiles but also for Jews, and thus for Jewish followers
of Jesus as well. One of these groups reached the conclusion that no real Jew
could possibly have written such negative things about the Torah. So they
fabricated an alternative biography of the apostle: He was born a Gentile
and converted to Judaism after falling in love with a Jewish woman. When
she spurned him, he turned his anger against Judaism and the Jewish law.
Here is the lesson: *While there are huge ideological and theological differences
among ancient readers of Paul, everyone, his "friends" and his "enemies" alike,
agreed on one issue: Paul preached that God had finally repudiated Judaism and
rejected the Jewish law.*

Now we encounter a paradox. How is it possible that the "apostle of the
heretics" wound up at the very center of the Christian New Testament? Of the
twenty-seven writings in the New Testament, thirteen claim Paul as their
author. The book of Acts is largely about Paul; one epistle, 2 Peter, speaks
about him; another, James, appears to have been written against him, or at least
against those who claimed to represent his views; the Letter to the Hebrews
was finally accepted into the New Testament canon due to the notion that it
was somehow connected to Paul; one of the Gospels, Luke, was traditionally
held to have been written under his influence. What brought about the
remarkable recovery of the "heretical apostle" from his (heretical) friends and
from his enemies (Jewish Christians)?

The answer is: the Paul of the New Testament. There we find him sand-
wiched between the book of Acts and the Pastoral Letters (1 and 2 Timothy,
Titus), each the product of a later generation of Christians. These later writings frame, and thus affect the presentation of, their mid-first-century subject.
One scholar describes the Paul of the New Testament in these terms: "The
price the Apostle of the Gentiles had to pay to be allowed to remain in the
church was the complete surrender of his personality and historical particu-

larity."[3] Here is the lesson: *In order to peer behind the domesticated image of Paul projected by his place in the New Testament, we will need to untie him from those moorings. We will need to read him in his own settings, in his own times, not as he was read later in totally new settings and times. The settings in which we place him determine how we interpret him.*

Before we jump into these troubled waters, I need to make one point clear. Rather than speak of "Christianity," I will use the term "the Jesus movement" to refer to Jesus' following in his own lifetime, in the lifetime of Paul, and for several decades thereafter. My reasons for this are straightforward: (1) Paul never uses the term "Christianity" himself, and seems to have no sense at all that he is establishing a new religion. (2) Even more important, using the term "Christianity" to label the early phase of what I will call the Jesus movement leads us to anachronism. What I mean by this is that we will almost surely read back into Paul's own time the opinions, debates, and circumstances that emerged only later on, long after Paul's period, when Christianity really did emerge as something distinct from and even opposed to Judaism. But in my view—and here I stand with many others—this separation did not happen until centuries after Paul's death. In speaking of the Jesus movement instead of Christianity, then, I want to avoid the serious mistake of reading later times and later views into earlier times and earlier views.

So what do we know about Paul in his own times and where do we look for information? His own letters are the obvious place to begin. For the record, and following academic consensus, I limit these to Romans, 1 and 2 Corinthians, Galatians, Philippians, Philemon, and 1 Thessalonians. The others— 2 Thessalonians, 1 and 2 Timothy, Titus, Colossians, Ephesians—were probably written in Paul's name by later followers (a normal and honorable practice in antiquity). The book of Acts contains lengthy narratives about Paul, and it is tempting to use it as a source of information about him. But the author's reliability comes into question because of the many points where his account confuses or even contradicts what we have in Paul's own letters. Scholars generally hold that most of Luke's information about Paul is suspect, unless confirmed by Paul himself.

One of the curiosities of Paul's letters is that he says so little about his own life. One important exception is the letter to the Philippians:

> Beware of the dogs, beware of the evil workers, beware of those who mutilate the flesh! . . . If anyone has reason to be confident in the flesh, I have more: circumcised on the eighth day, a member of the people of Israel, of the tribe of Benjamin, a Hebrew born of Hebrews; as to the law, a Pharisee; as to zeal [*zêlos*], a persecutor of the church [congregation (*ekklêsia*)]; as to righteousness under the law, [I was] blameless. (Phil. 3:2, 4b–6)

Paul is obviously angry here. But what is going on is fairly straightforward. Paul is under attack. In this passage he defends himself against what can only be called opponents *within the Jesus movement*. The "dogs," these other apostles, seem to have questioned Paul's Jewish credentials and thus the authority of his gospel. We will return to this issue later on. For now we need to focus on his response, which I can only characterize as an effort to present himself as a "super Jew." He calls himself a Pharisee (maybe it would be better to speak of him as an ex-Pharisee). In much of later Christian history, the Pharisees have acquired a terrible reputation, largely due to the negative and highly biased portrayal of them as enemies of Jesus in the Gospels. But for Paul, the label had once been a source of great pride and honor.

So, what did it mean to be a Pharisee in the first century? And what sort of Pharisee was Paul? These questions are easy to ask, but very difficult to answer. The chief reason for this is simple: Paul is one of only two Pharisees from the first century about whom we have any firsthand information at all. The other figure is the Jewish historian Josephus, Paul's somewhat younger contemporary. Josephus tells us a little about the Pharisees and also claims to have been a follower of the "rules of the Pharisees."[4] Josephus says that:

> Pharisees followed not only the written Torah (the five books of Moses), but also what he calls unwritten or oral traditions from the ancient past.
>
> Pharisees enjoyed considerable popularity among other Jews.[5]
>
> Pharisees lived frugally; they believed that God directs the course of history; and they anticipated a last judgment following the resurrection of the dead at the end of time.

From the Gospels' portrait of the Pharisees, we learn that they placed great emphasis on table fellowship, observed nonbiblical fast days, and gave tithes to the Temple in Jerusalem. Finally, (and here we come close to Paul), we learn that they actively sought converts: "Woe to you, scribes and Pharisees, hypocrites! For you cross sea and land to make a single convert [*prosêlutos*], and you make the new convert twice as much a child of hell as yourselves" (Matt. 23:15).

If we apply these characterizations of the Pharisees to Paul, we get a picture of someone who was highly educated in the Bible and who was skilled in various techniques of biblical interpretation. All of this certainly comes through clearly in the scriptural arguments of his letters, thereby attesting to his Pharisaic training. Beyond this, there are two other features of first-century Pharisaism that seem to have left their mark on Paul: the search for converts, and the anticipation of the end times.

I return for a moment to the passage in Matthew 23 about Pharisees and their efforts to make converts. Paul seems to have been this kind of Pharisee.

We know that as an apostle (the Greek word means someone who is "sent out") he devoted much of his life to bringing Gentiles into the Jesus movement. There is good reason to believe that even before his conversion or commissioning by the risen Christ he was actively engaged in making converts (*proselytoi*), that is, in bringing Gentiles into (Pharisaic) Judaism. Some scholars have argued that the Pharisees were seeking converts among their fellow Jews and not among Gentiles. This in my view seems unlikely, however, because the term "proselyte," in ancient Jewish texts written in Greek, almost always refers to a non-Jew who embraces Judaism.

The second feature of Pharisaic thought is the powerful stream of eschatological expectations and ecstatic religious experiences that cuts across all forms of Judaism at that time. Here, too, Paul was very much at home. Paul expected the end of history—which he associated with the Parousia, or second coming of Christ—in his own lifetime. It is not too much to insist that every feature of his activity as an apostle of Christ, including his mission to Gentiles, was shaped by his conviction that he was living in the final days. Consistent with his eschatological orientation, he claims to have made an ascent to the third heaven: "I know a person in Christ [=Paul] who fourteen years ago was caught up to the third heaven—whether in the body or out of the body I do not know; God knows" (2 Cor. 12:2). Paul reports several visual and auditory revelations from God and the resurrected Christ (1 Cor. 15:8; Gal. 1:15–16); he himself spoke in tongues (1 Cor. 14:18); and he was not reluctant to mention that he performed miracles (Rom. 15:19; 2 Cor. 12:12). These experiences and charismatic acts conform him to those eschatological and mystical forms of Judaism familiar to us from the Second Temple period.

While we are dealing with issues of education, we should also make note of another feature in Paul's Pharisaism that literally leaps from every page. He wrote in Greek! In fact, he is the only Pharisee we know of (though there were surely others) whose mother tongue was Greek. While he may have known Hebrew, and the Hebrew Bible, his native language and his habitual biblical text seem to have been Greek. What is more, his Greek is highly literate and reveals a comfortable familiarity with the conventions of Greek rhetoric. Somewhere along the way he must have learned how to make sophisticated arguments before a public audience. Paul puts this knowledge of rhetoric to work in all his letters. Here I will just mention that the rediscovery of Paul's level of Greek education ranks as one of the most important developments in recent Pauline studies and has brought about major changes in the ways we read his letters.[6] I say "rediscovery" because Paul's ancient Greek Christian readers would have been well aware of his rhetorical skills. Here is the lesson: *Just as we cannot hope to understand his letters without a deep knowledge of the Bible, so also if we are ignorant of his rhetorical techniques, when we read his letters we are bound to get him wrong.*

Back to our main theme, Paul the Pharisee. As part of his counterattack in the letter to the Philippians, Paul portrays himself as having been something of an extremist, a zealot. Not only was his righteousness—that is, his ability to live up to the commands of the Torah—"blameless," but as part of his piety he includes the remarkable admission that he had been a persecutor of the Jesus movement, not despite his piety but precisely because of it. It is important to note that this passage from Philippians 3 gives the lie to a long tradition of Christian and Jewish interpreters who have claimed that Paul abandoned the Torah because he experienced it as a terrible burden. Unless we are prepared to dismiss this passage altogether, we will have to give up the notion that Paul left the Torah, as interpreted by the Pharisees, in favor of Christ because he felt guilty at his inability to live up to its impossible demands. On this point, he is as clear as he can be: "As to my observance of the law, I was blameless!"

Here we must add a word or two about his use of the term "zeal," *zelos* in Greek. Recall that Paul illustrates his zeal by pointing to his former persecutions of the followers of Jesus. He thereby places himself in a long line of biblical and postbiblical figures who stood ready to defend their convictions about living according to the Torah against those, whether Jews or outsiders, who threatened to undermine them. Thus it seems fair to infer that Paul persecuted other Jews in the early Jesus movement because he saw in it some fundamental threat to his vision of Judaism. But what did this persecution involve, and what actions did he take? At a minimum, we can assume that he succeeded in expelling some of Jesus' Jewish followers from local synagogues, in hauling them before local Jewish courts, and in seeing to it that they were given the same punishment that he experienced himself later on, as an apostle of Christ—namely, the disciplinary lashing that he mentions in 2 Corinthians: "Five times I have received from the Jews the forty lashes minus one" (11:24).[7]

Some interpreters have tried to minimize the intensity of Paul's attacks against the Jesus movement, but his own language suggests otherwise. He says that he undertook to destroy the community. Indeed, he is quite forthright about his actions against the followers of Jesus: "You have heard, no doubt, of my earlier life in Judaism. I was violently persecuting the *ecclesia* of God and was trying to destroy it. I advanced in Judaism beyond many among my people of the same age, for I was far more zealous for the traditions of my ancestors" (Gal. 1:13–14).

Here we run headlong into a major difficulty. What was it about the Jesus movement that led the zealous Pharisee to see it as a major threat to his view of Judaism and of the Torah? Unfortunately, Paul does not tell us; without evidence, we must speculate. Scholars have proposed a number of possible explanations. Perhaps Paul found the idea of a crucified messiah to be offensive. Paul tells us that some Jews found the idea unacceptable: "But we proclaim [a/the] Christ[Messiah] crucified, a stumbling block to Jews and foolishness to Gentiles" (1 Cor. 1:23). That a crucified man should be called the Messiah seemed foolish to most Jews, but this was hardly a justification for persecution. Or perhaps he was reacting to the divisive impact that Jesus' followers caused in local synagogues, which some scholars think is evinced in the Gospel of John, which speaks of an expulsion of "Christ confessors" from the synagogue (9:22, 12:42, 16:2).

Or was Paul protesting against those currents in the early Jesus movement that attacked the sanctity of the Jerusalem Temple when they argued that it was not really the dwelling place of God?[8] Or was there something about the way that Jews in the Jesus movement were dealing with Gentile followers of Jesus? Perhaps they allowed Gentiles into full membership in the church by converting them to Judaism, without expecting them to keep the commands of the Torah. We do know that after his conversion Paul argued strenuously against the view that some within the movement had adopted as the official policy toward Gentile believers: that they could convert fully, receive circumcision, and thus become members of Israel but not be expected to make a full effort to live according to the commandments. To this Paul objects: "Once again I testify to every man who lets himself be circumcised that he is obliged to obey the entire law" (Gal. 5:3).

Clearly, there are problems with each one of these proposals, and my own view is that it is a mistake to look for a single cause. In surveying the explanations just cited, we may find the best clue in a brief passage in Josephus, who mentions the death of James, the brother of Jesus:

> He [Ananus, the Jewish high priest] convened the judges of the San-
> hedrin [a Jewish high court] and brought before them a man named
> James, the brother of Jesus who was called the Christ, and certain oth-
> ers. He accused them of having transgressed the law and delivered
> them to be stoned. Those of the inhabitants of the city who were con-
> sidered most fair-minded and who were strict in observance of the law
> were offended at this.[9]

This passage accuses James of transgressing the law/Torah, though no specifics are given, while it portrays those whom Josephus describes as fair-minded and observant as being opposed to the action taken by Ananus. If Paul's hostility to the Jesus movement was at all like that of Ananus, then he was probably regarded as an intemperate hothead even by his fellow Jews. Indeed, we know that Paul saw himself in much the same light, for, as we have noted, he describes himself as "advanced in Judaism" and "*zealous for the traditions of my ancestors*" (Gal. 1:14; emphasis mine).

Surely there were several factors at work in Paul's actions both before and after his conversion. This much seems certain: both before his conversion and after, following Christ and obedience to the Torah stood as mutually exclusive values in Paul's heart and mind. His zealous loyalty to the Torah initially led him to oppose Christ. Later, his commitment to Christ led him to denigrate the Torah. But there is a third factor in this picture: the Gentiles. This factor is almost always forgotten or ignored by modern interpreters. The Gentiles represent the pivot on which the axis of Christ and Torah rotate. What Paul the persecutor held against the Jesus movement was not that they admitted Gentiles as members—not at all—but rather that they admitted Gentiles without demanding full acceptance of or responsibility for the Torah. Conversely, after his conversion he did denigrate the Torah, but only in relation to Gentiles. After his conversion, Christ and Torah remained polar opposites and the pivotal issue remained Gentiles. The center of his new gospel was the redemption of Gentiles by Christ—not by its polar opposite, observance of the Torah. Once the axis rotated 180 degrees, Christ replaced Torah as the gateway to salvation, *not* for Jews but for Gentiles.

All of this brings us to what was clearly the central event in Paul's life, his transformation from persecutor of the church to apostle of Jesus Christ. Here I need to be blunt. There has been more nonsense written about Paul's conversion than on just about any topic I can think of. The standard view is that Paul converted from Judaism to Christianity, that he abandoned Torah for Christ, and that he created the rejection-replacement view that characterizes Christian anti-Judaism. But if others and I are right in saying that there was no Christianity as such in Paul's time, he *cannot* have converted to Christianity. As one Jewish interpreter has put it, "Paul did not become a Christian since there were no Christians in those times."[10]

Furthermore, a study of the broad range of conversion stories and experiences reveals that most conversions take place within a single religious tradition; only a small number involve a movement into something radically new. A good modern analogy comes from the political realm: the Marxist who becomes a political conservative is a good example of what I have in mind. Here the parallel with Paul is quite close, for the Marxist, like Paul, has an underlying mind-set that reveals a set of polar opposites (socialism against capitalism). When the conversion is complete, the poles are simply reversed. No new elements enter the system. Capitalism was never foreign to the Marxist, but always a central (negative) element. But what was positive before becomes negative and what was negative before becomes positive. Paul speaks in words that sound very much like this:

> Yet whatever gains I had, these I have come to regard as loss because of Christ. More than that, I regard everything as loss because of the

surpassing value of knowing Christ Jesus my Lord. For his sake I have
suffered the loss of all things, and I regard them as rubbish, in order
that I may gain Christ. (Phil. 3:7–8)

There is no doubt that Paul's conversion was a dramatic turning point in
his life. And it brought with it dramatic consequences, for him and for subsequent history. Let's take a look at some of these consequences, keeping in mind
the bipolar structure of Torah and Christ, with Gentiles in the middle.

First, Paul came to think of himself from that point on as the divinely
appointed apostle of Christ to the Gentiles. It is not just that he always refers
to himself as the apostle to the Gentiles, which is true. It is not just that he
always addresses his letters to Gentile communities, which he does. Beyond
this, he identifies the very essence of his own conversion with his mission to
the Gentiles: "God . . . was pleased to reveal his Son to me, so that I might
proclaim him among the Gentiles" (Gal. 1:15–16). "Nevertheless on some
points I have written to you rather boldly by way of reminder, because of the
grace given me by God to be a minister of Christ Jesus to the Gentiles in the
priestly service of the gospel of God, so that the offering of the Gentiles may
be acceptable" (Rom. 15:15–16).

Second, Paul's status or his calling as the apostle to the Gentiles was not just
one feature among others in his conversion: it was its very center. If he had
already been active as a Pharisaic missionary to Gentiles on behalf of the
Torah, then what really changed was not his target audience but his message—
no longer Gentiles and Torah but now Gentiles and Christ. Furthermore, his
message was not just *to* Gentiles, it was *about* Gentiles. As Paul reiterates frequently, his gospel stated that Gentiles were saved through faith in Jesus
Christ. Practically speaking, what this meant was that he traveled and taught
throughout the eastern Mediterranean, preaching his gospel to and about the
redemption of the Gentiles in the last days of history.

A third consequence of his conversion is that he undertook a profound
rereading of his Bible—what we have come to call the Old Testament, but
what for him was simply the Scriptures. Suddenly, it became clear to him that
all the biblical promises regarding the salvation of the Gentiles had been fulfilled in Christ. God's repeated promises to Abraham in the book of Genesis—
that through Abraham the nations of the world would be blessed (12:3)—serve
as the foundation of Paul's argument that Christ represents the fulfillment of
these promises, and thus that Paul's gospel had been present in Scripture from
the very beginning:

> As for me, this is my covenant with you: You shall be the ancestor of
> a multitude of nations. No longer shall your name be Abram, but
> your name shall be Abraham; for I have made you the ancestor of a

> multitude of nations. I will make you exceedingly fruitful; and I will make nations of you, and kings shall come from you. (Gen. 17:4–6; cf. 12: 2–3; 18:18)

In this passage, Paul saw a double reference to his mission to the Gentiles: "nations" (=Gentiles) + Abraham's descendants, which he took to mean not just Jews but Gentiles too. Stanley Stowers has argued that Paul repeatedly explains the gospel and God's righteousness by referring to the story of the Abrahamic promise concerning the Gentiles.[11] In other words, for Paul, God's righteousness apart from the law means, specifically, God's redemption of the Gentiles.

Finally, Paul's conversion/transformation led to persistent and bitter opposition to him and his mission from within the Jesus movement itself. We have no difficulty imagining that from the very beginning his claim to be an apostle of Christ must have been hugely controversial. After all, was this not the same Paul who had tried to destroy the church? Imagine yourself for a moment as a Torah-observant Jesus follower receiving word that Paul was no longer a persecutor of the church, but an apostle of Christ! Now add to this the view in the early Jesus movement that in order to become a member of the community, Gentiles had to become Jews and therefore Gentile males had to undergo the rite of circumcision. In this setting, Paul's gospel must have made his presence seem all the more intolerable.

We know that Paul's opponents within the Jesus movement undertook an active mission against him. They followed him from place to place, trying to undo his preaching. They attacked his credentials as a Jew; they pointed to his earlier work as a persecutor of the church; they questioned his conversion story; and they tried in every way possible to undermine his gospel. These opponents met with some success. What we read in his letters—especially Galatians, Philippians, and 2 Corinthians—is Paul's bitter counterattack, an attack, I repeat, against anti-Pauline Jewish apostles *within* the Jesus movement. To get a measure of just how heated these battles could be, listen to some of Paul's scorching rhetoric:

> You foolish Galatians! Who has bewitched you? (Gal. 3:1)

> Beware of the dogs, beware of the evil workers, beware of those who mutilate the flesh! (Phil. 3:2)

> I wish those who unsettle you [by insisting on circumcision] would slip and mutilate themselves [by severing their own genitals!]. (Gal. 5:12)

The identity of these opponents is not clear. At the beginning of the controversy, the leaders of the Jesus movement in Jerusalem (Paul names them as

James the brother of Jesus, Cephas=Peter, and John) accepted Paul's gospel and mission as legitimate. Paul was free to preach to the Gentiles without requiring circumcision. But very soon this agreement broke down. Paul mentions certain "false brethren" and "certain men from James" who began their campaign against him. Whether James and the other leaders in Jerusalem, like Peter, changed their minds is uncertain. All that we can know for sure is that Paul's opponents claimed the authority of these "pillars," and that, in Galatians, Paul did too.

As for Peter, who was party to the original agreement in Jerusalem, he seems to have wavered under pressure from Paul's opponents. In Antioch he refused to eat with Gentiles within the new movement, and even Paul's coworker Barnabas collapsed under the pressure. Paul understood this to represent a reversal of the agreement reached earlier in Jerusalem. Thanks to the letter to the Galatians, we are able to eavesdrop on a truly remarkable confrontation between two lions of the early Jesus movement, Peter and Paul. After Peter's change of heart, Paul claims, he confronted Peter face-to-face and accused him of hypocrisy and betrayal: Peter had earlier agreed to eat with Gentiles, but now had changed his mind.

> When James and Cephas [= Peter] and John, who were acknowledged pillars, recognized the grace that had been given to me, they gave to Barnabas and me the right hand of fellowship, agreeing that we should go to the Gentiles and they to the circumcised. They asked only one thing, that we remember the poor, which was actually what I was eager to do. But when Cephas came to Antioch, I opposed him to his face, because he stood self-condemned; for until certain people came from James, he used to eat with the Gentiles. But after they came, he drew back and kept himself separate for fear of the circumcision faction. And the other Jews joined him in this hypocrisy, so that even Barnabas was led astray by their hypocrisy. (Gal. 2:9–13)

This is the last we hear of the dispute from Paul. But we know from later sources (Tertullian and various Jewish Christian texts) that the bitterness did not subside quickly; indeed, it continued long after Paul's death. For, as we have seen above, circles of Torah-observant believers—those who will come to be called Jewish Christians—spoke bitterly of Paul and of his mission for hundreds of years thereafter. What has survived from these early disputes is the image of Paul as the father of Christian anti-Judaism and the creator of the rejection-replacement theology that has reigned supreme from antiquity to the present.

Despite Christian tradition's adherence to this view, its major difficulties have long been recognized: each and every one of the statements in the preceding paragraph can be countered by another Pauline statement to the contrary. To illustrate these apparent contradictions, let us consider two sets of texts drawn from his letters. One set (*a*) consists of anti-Israel, anti-circumcision, or anti-law passages; the other (*b*), of pro-Israel, pro-circumcision, or pro-law passages.

   a) The Anti-Israel Set:

      "For all who rely on the works of the law are under a curse." (Gal. 3:10)

      "Now it is evident that no one is justified before God by the law" (Gal. 3:11)

      "For neither circumcision nor uncircumcision is anything; but a new creation is everything!" (Gal. 6:15)

      "For 'no human being will be justified in his sight' by deeds prescribed by the law, for through the law comes the knowledge of sin." (Rom. 3:20)

      "Israel, who did strive for the righteousness that is based on the law, did not succeed in fulfilling that law." (Rom. 9:31)

      "As regards the gospel they are enemies of God for your sake." (Rom. 11:28)

      "But their minds were hardened. Indeed, to this very day, when they hear the reading of the old covenant, that same veil is still there, since only in Christ is it set aside. Indeed, to this very day whenever Moses is read, a veil lies over their minds; but when one turns to the Lord, the veil is removed." (2 Cor. 3:14–16)

   b) The Pro-Israel Set:

      "What advantage has the Jew? Or what is the value of circumcision? Much in every way." (Rom. 3:1–2)

      "Do we then overthrow the law through this faith? By no means! On the contrary, we uphold the law." (Rom. 3:31)

      "What then should we say? That the law is sin? By no means!" (Rom. 7:7)

      "So the law is holy, and the commandment is holy and just and good." (Rom. 7:12)

      "They are Israelites, and to them belong the adoption, the glory, the covenants, the giving of the law, the worship, and the promises; to them belong the patriarchs, and from them, according to the flesh, comes the Messiah." (Rom. 9:4–5)

      "Is the law then opposed to the promises of God? Certainly not!" (Gal. 3:21)

      "Has God rejected his people? By no means!" (Rom. 11:1)

      "All Israel will be saved." (Rom. 11:26)

Now the problem emerges. Point by point, the two sets appear to contradict each other:

    Circumcision is of great value; *it counts for nothing.*

The law is holy; *it places its followers under a curse and cannot justify them before God.*

All Israel will be saved; *they are the enemies and have failed to fulfill their own law.*

Here is a major dilemma for all readers of Paul. No one wants an apostle riddled with contradictions. While many readers simply ignore the problem, acting as if the pro-Israel passages simply do not exist, most intelligent readers fall into the category of what I call the "contradictionists," who recognize and admit the tensions between the two sets of passages. Among contradictionist readers, one finds a variety of techniques for resolving these tensions. Some assign the contradictory passages to Paul's own unresolved feelings about Judaism following his conversion; others remove the offending passages, arguing that they were inserted by later editors who little understood Paul's thought; still others give up and conclude that he was simply incapable of straightforward, consistent thinking. By far the most common technique has been to subordinate one set of passages (always the pro-Israel set) and to insist that the anti-Israel passages represent his true thought.

Until recently, few have bothered to consider an even more radical solution to these difficulties, namely, that the apparent inconsistencies of Paul's letters might be located not in him but in his later readers, who read him through the lens of later Christian anti-Judaism. Why is it, I have often asked myself, that no one has tried to begin with the pro-Israel texts and to see how the anti-Israel passages can be made to fit in? Put differently: Why has no one wondered whether it might be possible to construct a different picture of Paul's teachings on the law and Israel by doing full justice to both sets of passages, without convicting him of contradictory thinking or subjecting his letters to radical excisions or to pop psychology?

In my view, this solution is not only possible; rather, it is the only approach that makes sense of what we know about Paul, his letters, and his times. Beginning with the pro-Israel passages, I argue that Paul need not, indeed cannot, be read according to the contradictionists. He is entirely innocent of all charges lodged against him by his anti-Jewish interpreters:

He was not the father of Christian anti-Judaism.

He was not the inventor of the rejection-replacement theory.

He did not repudiate the law of Moses.

He did not argue that God had rejected Israel.

Neither his enemies nor his audience in general were from outside the Jesus movement.

He did not expect Jews to find their salvation through Jesus Christ.

He was not a convert *from* Judaism or *to* Christianity.

As we have seen above, students of the early Jesus movement have long known that anti-Pauline apostles within the Jesus movement followed him from town to town, trying to impose their gospel of circumcision on his Gentile believers. The clearest example of their view appears in a brief passage from Acts: "Certain individuals [i.e., fellow Jesus-believers] came down from Judea [to Antioch] and were teaching the brothers, 'Unless you are circumcised according to the custom of Moses, you cannot be saved.'" Here we need to remind ourselves of what was at stake in this dispute. The issue was not *whether* Gentiles could become followers of Jesus. They could. On this issue both Paul and Paul's opponents were in agreement. What divided them was the question of whether Gentiles had first to become Jews or whether, as Paul insisted, a new way for Gentile believers had been opened up by the death of Jesus and faith in him—a way, as he puts it in his letter to the Romans, apart from the law, although he is quick to add that the Law and the Prophets bear witness to it (Rom. 3:21).

I must repeat here that all of this has long been understood by students of the early Jesus movement. But until recently students of Paul have been slow to recognize that it is precisely these anti-Pauline apostles—again, within the Jesus movement—who are the targets of his anger in Galatians and Philippians. His negative statements about circumcision have nothing to do with Jews outside the Jesus movement. Once we adopt these facts as our starting point for reading the letters, it becomes clear that, as the apostle to the Gentiles, Paul is focused exclusively on disputes about the law and circumcision of Gentiles *within the Jesus movement*. Everything in his letters (at least those like Romans, Galatians, and Philippians) is directed toward preserving the independence and the validity of his law-free gospel to and about Gentiles. Here is the lesson: *The image of Paul as the father of Christian anti-Judaism has no foundation in his letters.*

What happens to the traditional anti-Israel view of Paul if we take *these* facts and *these* settings as starting points for reading his letters? First, it becomes clear that Paul's exclusive concern as the apostle to the Gentiles was the new redeemed status of Gentiles-in-Christ, *not* the continuing status of Israel. This was his gospel, as he states time and time again. In other words, Gentiles were not only the target audience of his gospel, they were also its core message. Thus when we read his letters we should always ask as our first question, "How does this passage apply to his work with Gentiles?" One scholar has put the issue in this way: "Paul writes to Gentile Christians, dealing with Gentile-Christian problems. It is remarkable that in the endless discussion of Paul's understanding of the law, few have asked what a first-century Jew would have thought about the law *as it relates to Gentiles.*"[12]

In an effort to demonstrate how this new way of thinking might clarify Paul's letters, I propose to examine a small sample of passages that have traditionally been taken as manifesting Paul's anti-Judaism. The sample will emphasize the same passages cited earlier in the now so-called "anti-Israel set."

> For all who rely on the works of the law are under a curse. . . . Now it is evident that no one is justified before God by the law. (Gal. 3:10–11)

> For "no human being will be justified in his [God's] sight" by deeds prescribed by the law, for through the law comes the knowledge of sin. (Rom. 3:20)

These two passages have served for many centuries as proof texts for the view that Paul had come, after his conversion, to see the Torah in a totally negative light. The law could no longer lead anyone, Jew or Gentile, to redemption. The phrase "works of the law" has been taken as an exact equivalent of "Torah" or "law of Moses," and the persons spoken of are always assumed to be Jews. But a careful reading of the passages fails to sustain such an interpretation.

In Galatians, it is clear that Paul is addressing Jesus-believers who were Gentiles, not Jews; he is describing *their* situation, not that of Jews. His argument is twofold. First, the condition of Gentiles, and only of Gentiles, before Christ was one of curse, slavery, and spiritual death. By now abandoning Paul's teachings and gospel, these Gentile believers are in danger of reverting to their former condition—outside the law and thus cursed, enslaved, and spiritually dead again. Second, as he insists here and elsewhere, by undergoing circumcision while at the same time failing to assume full responsibility for the law of Moses, they are placing themselves under the curse of Deuteronomy (Gal. 3:10 cites Deut. 27:26—"Cursed be anyone who does not uphold the words of this law by observing them"). As the entire letter makes plain, Paul's opponents were urging circumcision on male believers, in accordance with the view expressed in Acts 15:1 ("Unless you are circumcised according to the custom of Moses, you cannot be saved"), but not requiring that they fully observe the laws. As Paul reiterates in Galatians 5:3, arguing forcefully against his opponents and those who had fallen under their spell, "I testify to every man who lets himself be circumcised that he is obliged to obey the entire law." It now becomes apparent that the key phrase "works of the law" describes this very situation—Jesus-believers of Gentile origin who were engaged in limited and selective observance of the laws of Moses following their circumcision.

The passage in Romans 3 introduces another opportunity for serious mis-reading. It has long been assumed that in Romans 3 Paul claims that Jews believed that they were justified before God by virtue of observing the law. Thus Paul repudiates Judaism as a religion of works righteousness. The diffi-culty with this view, as derived from Romans 3, is again twofold. First, no Jew ever held such a view. The law or observance of it did not justify the Jew; God did. Living according to the law was rather the Jew's response to God's gra-cious acts that founded the nation: choosing Israel, bringing them from slav-ery to freedom, giving them the Torah, and bringing them into the land. Second, as the immediately following verses make clear (Rom. 3:21—"But now, apart from the law, the righteousness of God has been disclosed"), Paul is here talking about Gentiles and their inclusion, at the end of history, in the promises of God. Thus the law produces sin not in Jews but in Gentiles, because they stand condemned outside the law, literally as outlaws.[13] But all of that has now changed. Gentile Jesus-believers now stand on an equal footing with Jews as beneficiaries of God's saving grace, but in a different mode. The entire letter to the Romans is about the inclusion of Gentiles, not the exclu-sion of Jews. "Is God the God of Jews only? Is he not the God of Gentiles also?" (Rom. 3:29). "Is this blessedness [of Abraham], then, pronounced only on the circumcised, or also on the uncircumcised [Gentiles]?" (Rom. 4:9).

> For neither circumcision nor uncircumcision is anything; but a new
> creation is everything! (Gal. 6:15)

This passage has also served to buttress the anti-Israel view of Paul. Here, it is alleged, Paul rejects circumcision and, by extension, the entire Jewish law. But, as we have already seen, the letter to the Galatians is about Gentile Jesus-believers who have, from Paul's point of view, been misled into adopting cir-cumcision and partial observance of the Torah. The result for them, as he argues throughout, is disastrous—curse, slavery, and spiritual death once again. The point of this passage is simply that circumcision is no longer relevant in any way for Gentiles. Something new has happened for Gentiles: Jesus Christ. They, not the Jews, have been rescued from their former predicament. They, not the Jews, are a new creation. As if to confirm this reading, Paul proclaims in Romans that circumcision remains fully valid for Jews. "What advantage has the Jew? Or what is the value of circumcision [for Jews]? Much in every way" (Rom. 3:1–2).

> Israel, who did strive for the righteousness that is based on the law, did
> not succeed in fulfilling that law. (Rom. 9:31)

Here again we find a text used to demonstrate that ancient Jews believed that they were made righteous by their own act of observing the law. Once again Jews are accused of following a religion of works righteousness. But we now understand that such a view is completely unhistorical and indefensible. Jews held no such view. Furthermore, as we have seen earlier, Paul's use of the term "righteousness" (*dikaiosunê* in Greek) always carries a very specific meaning in his letters. God's righteousness designates his promise to redeem the Gentiles. Thus the point made in Romans 9:31 is not that Israel's observance was mistaken, but that Israel failed to understand God's plan to redeem the Gentiles through Jesus Christ. Stowers summarizes Paul's argument as follows: "Instead of accepting God's way of extending his righteousness on the basis of Abraham's and Jesus' faithfulness, Jews have insisted that gentiles perform works of the law."[14]

> For Christ is the end of the law so that there may be righteousness for everyone who believes. (Rom. 10:4)

Here is another pillar in the edifice of the anti-Israel image of Paul. The Greek word translated here as "end" is *telos*. The customary interpretation has been that Paul here announces the end, the termination, the cancellation of the law. But the ordinary meaning of *telos* is "goal," or "purpose," or "intention." Paul's point is that a proper understanding of Scripture—of course, this means understanding Scripture in Paul's terms—shows that God had intended from the very beginning to redeem the Gentiles through Jesus Christ. This is precisely how Paul interprets biblical passages throughout his letters: their *telos* is Jesus Christ and the redemption of the Gentiles. This is what Jews have failed to understand. Their error is not in observing the law but in failing to see that what has happened was predicted long ago in Scripture. As he puts it in Romans 3:21, "Now, apart from the law, the righteousness of God [=his plan to redeem the Gentiles through Jesus Christ] has been disclosed, and *is attested by the law and the prophets*" (emphasis mine). And we should add that the phrase "apart from the law" here means only that a new way has been opened up for Gentiles, not, as the traditional view holds, that this new way cancels the old way of Israel.

> As regards the gospel they are enemies of God for your sake. (Rom. 11:28)

Romans 9–11 belongs to Paul's attempt to correct what he takes to be a profound misreading of his views about Israel and the Torah, or law of Moses. Apparently some Gentiles in the Jesus movement had taken him to be an advocate of what we have called the rejection-replacement view, namely, that the Jews and their law had been rejected by God and that the Jews had been replaced as the chosen people by Gentile followers of Christ. In Romans 9–11 Paul repudiates this view in the clearest possible terms:

> To [the Israelites] belong the sonship, the glory, the covenants, the
> giving of the law, the worship, and the promises; to them belong the
> patriarchs, and from them, according to the flesh, comes the Messiah.
> (Rom. 9:4–5 RSV)

> Has God rejected his people? By no means! (Rom. 11:1)

> All Israel will be saved. (Rom. 11:26)

At the same time, Paul lays out an elaborate scenario according to which God has temporarily caused Israel to stumble *so that the Gentiles could be brought into the promises*. In other words, the cause of Israel's momentary stumbling has nothing to do with any wrongdoing on Israel's part. Instead it is an essential element in God's provisional plan, foreknown to the prophets and most recently to Paul, in order to bring salvation to the Gentiles. Paul himself, well aware of the unusual nature of this idea, calls it a mystery (Rom. 11:25). He continues, "A hardening has come upon part of Israel, until the full number of the Gentiles has come in. And so *all Israel will be saved*" (vv. 25–26, emphasis mine). Here we must note that Paul says that "all Israel will be saved." He does not say, "All Israel will have faith in Christ" or "All Israel will become Christian." Virtually all commentators on the passage render it in this latter form, but that is simply not what Paul says—nor, therefore, what he means. Paul never speaks of Israel's redemption in terms of Christ. Just as he no longer thinks of salvation for Gentiles within the Mosaic covenant, so he does not imagine salvation for Jews as occurring through their acceptance of Jesus Christ.

Thus our passage in Romans 11:28 finds a clear meaning. As part of God's plan, most of Israel has for a short time become an "enemy" of the gospel. That is, most of Israel has not taken Paul's view of things, in order that the Gentiles might come in ("for your sake"). But, and this is essential for Paul, in the very near future the plan will be accomplished and "all Israel will be saved." The notion that this passage speaks of Israel's permanent rejection is simply untenable. It is only later readers, overlooking both the intensity of Paul's eschatological commitment and the details of the "mystery" in chapter 11, who import the idea of Israel's permanent rejection.

> To this very day, when they hear the reading of the old covenant, that
> same veil is still there, since only in Christ is it set aside. Indeed, to this
> very day whenever Moses is read, a veil lies over their minds. (2 Cor.
> 3:14–15)

Here is another pillar of the anti-Jewish Paul. On this view, Paul is talking about Israel, the Jews, although everything else in the letter concerns the

Corinthian believers themselves. He is thus assumed to be accusing Israel of blindness and of an inability to understand their own Scriptures because a metaphorical veil obscures their vision. But a number of recent interpreters have reversed this reading. Following the principle that one should always look close to home to find the targets of angry language, these interpreters locate Paul's Corinthian enemies, those who are incapable of properly understanding Scripture, *inside* the Jesus movement. As one critic puts it, "It is not Israel that Paul attacks but his opponents in Corinth."[15] In many ways, the situation in Corinth is like that in Galatia and Philippi: opponents of Paul *within the Jesus movement* have attacked Paul's credentials and succeeded in persuading members of his congregation to follow a path different from his. In the process, they have used biblical interpretations to support their position. Here, as in Galatians and Philippians, Paul fights back. His basic argument is that the opponents hold a faulty view of Scripture, by which he means, of course, that they hold a view other than his.

From our brief analysis of these passages emerges what I have called the new view of Paul, not as the father of Christian anti-Judaism, not as a critic of Israel, and not as one who rejected the law of Moses for Jews. I must admit that virtually all subsequent interpreters have read him in just the opposite fashion. If I am right, this misreading began already in his own lifetime. Paul shows a clear awareness of it in his letter to the Romans. But he is as clear as anyone can be that this was not his position: "Circumcision indeed is of value if you obey the law" (Rom. 2:25). And there is more. He never speaks of Gentiles (those whom we anachronistically call "Christians") as replacing Israel, or of God as having rejected Israel in favor of a new chosen people. I cannot deny that virtually every subsequent interpreter has read him in just this way, but I must emphasize that Paul had already vehemently repudiated this misreading and sought to correct it in his letter to the Romans: "I ask, then, has God rejected his people [Israel]? By no means!" (Rom. 11:1).

Finally, Paul never speaks of Israel's redemption in terms of Christ. Just as he no longer thinks of salvation for Gentiles within the Mosaic covenant, so he does not imagine salvation for Jews through Christ. Further, and significantly, Paul expected all these things to be accomplished in his own lifetime. It was the failure of the "end" to come as anticipated that turned his arguments, originally directed against competing factions *within the Jesus movement*, into arguments against Israel and the Torah. Here, then, is the final lesson: *Once we recover the original circumstances of his letters and reread them within those settings, the old view of the anti-Jewish Paul becomes impossible to defend.*

NOTES

1. M. Wiles, *The Divine Apostle: The Interpretation of St. Paul's Epistles in the Early Church* (Cambridge: Cambridge University Press, 1967), pp. 132–39.
2. Krister Stendahl, *Paul among Jews and Gentiles* (Philadelphia: Fortress Press, 1976), p. 86f.
3. Walter Bauer, *Orthodoxy and Heresy in Earliest Christianity* (Philadelphia: Fortress Press, 1971), p. 227.
4. Josephus's chief reports about the Pharisees appear in *Life* 11–15; *Jewish War* 2.159–168; *Jewish Antiquities* 18.11–16.
5. It is worth noting that, despite Josephus's remark about their widespread popularity, the Pharisees were not well regarded in all circles of ancient Judaism. They are roundly denounced in the famous "Woes" of Matthew 23 and are generally, though not always, portrayed as enemies of Jesus in the Gospels. In his book *Jesus* (Jerusalem: Magnes Press, 1998), David Flusser notes that the "term 'Pharisee' in Hebrew usually bore a negative connotation. In those days, if one said 'Pharisee,' one immediately thought of a religious hypocrite" (p. 69). Flusser refers to passages in the Babylonian Talmud (*Sotah* 22b) and the Dead Sea Scrolls (*Damascus Document* 8.12; 19.25).
6. See in particular the work of Stanley Stowers, *A Rereading of Romans: Justice, Jews, & Gentiles* (New Haven, Conn.: Yale University Press, 1994).
7. On the issues underlying these traditional Jewish punishments, see Paula Fredriksen, "Judaism, the Circumcision of Gentiles, and Apocalyptic Hope: Another Look at Galatians 1 and 2," *Journal of Theological Studies* 42 (1991): 532–64.
8. It is worth noting that other groups took the opposite view, namely, that God did dwell in the Temple; see the saying attributed to Jesus in Matthew 23:21, "Whoever swears by the sanctuary, swears by it and by the one who dwells in it."
9. Josephus, *Jewish Antiquities* 20.200.
10. Pinchas Lapide, in Lapide and P. Stuhlmacher, *Paul, Rabbi and Apostle* (Minneapolis: Augsburg, 1984), p. 47.
11. Stowers, *Rereading Romans*, p. 307.
12. Lloyd Gaston, *Paul and the Torah* (Vancouver: University of British Columbia Press, 1987), p. 23.
13. See the extensive argument in Stowers, *Rereading*, pp. 176–93.
14. Ibid., p. 286.
15. H. Ulonska, "Die Doxa des Mose," *Evangelische Theologie* 26 (1966): 385. Other interpreters who have taken the same view include L. Gaston, *Paul and the Torah*, pp. 150–68; Dieter Georgi, *The Opponents of Paul in Second Corinthians* (Philadelphia: Fortress Press, 1986), pp. 315–19; and J. F. Collange, *Énigmes de la deuxième Épître de Paul aux Corinthiens: Étude exégétique de 2 Cor. 2:14-7:4* (Cambridge: Cambridge University Press, 1972).

4

Matthew, Mark, and Luke:
Good News or Bad?

Amy-Jill Levine

Are the Gospels and the Acts of the Apostles anti-Jewish? This question cannot be answered with a simple yes or no. Passages that sound "pro-Jewish" to some ears will sound anti-Jewish to others. To give but one example: For an interfaith service here in Nashville, a minister proposed a reading from Matthew's Gospel that asks, "Why are you concerned about what you eat, or what you wear?" (6:25–34). Spoken by Jesus, a Jew who kept the dietary laws given in the Torah and who wore the fringes (Hebrew: *tzitzit*) that Numbers 15:37–41 commands all Jewish men to wear, the statement poetically exhorts the listener to avoid anything that interferes with faithful living. Spoken by a Christian minister to a group that includes Jews—Jews who keep *kashruth* (the dietary laws), Jews who wear *tzitziot*—the line easily sounds like a criticism of Jewish practice.

This example illustrates two elements that complicate the answer to our initial question. One is the fact that many New Testament passages can be read and interpreted in a variety of different, even contradictory, ways. The second is the conviction that historical study will acquit the New Testament of the charges of anti-Judaism. Many people, scholars and the general public alike, believe that if we could only understand the specific historical situations from which those texts arose and to which they were addressed, we would be able to show that the Gospels and Acts are not at heart anti-Jewish. Alas, what an evangelist sought to suggest about the relationship between those Jews and Gentiles who proclaimed Jesus the Messiah and those Jews—the vast majority—who did not can never be determined definitively by historical research, no matter how rigorous.

We can at best make educated guesses concerning the communities within which the texts were written. We can only speculate about how, why, and to what degree particular passages, as well as the overall narrative, were originally perceived to be anti-Jewish. Because these texts were read aloud and then interpreted by local or visiting teachers, the impression each text gave necessarily varied, depending on performance and interpretation. Moreover, there can easily be a gap between what one person says or writes and the message that someone else receives.

Jesus himself was a Jew speaking to other Jews. His teachings comport with the tradition of Israel's prophets. Judaism has always had a self-critical component, and its concerns for social justice and wholehearted worship have been sounded in Jewish Scripture and tradition throughout the centuries. Of course, Judaism is not alone in valuing prophetic voice: all religious groups need occasional wake-up calls. Christian history has seen numerous critics, ranging from Catherine of Sienna and Francis of Assisi to Luther, Calvin, and Wesley, to John XXIII and Martin Luther King Jr. The self-critical impulse can also be seen in church revivals, and in demands for justice within both church and society at large. The potential for danger—in the case we are considering here, for anti-Judaism—arises when the Scriptures of one group (the Jews) become the Scriptures of a second group (the Christians). In such a case, the positive portrayal of God's people can all too easily be taken by Christian readers to refer to themselves, whereas the self-criticism can be taken to refer to the Jews only.

I sometimes imagine discussing these matters with the evangelists themselves. On reading Matthew 27:25, I ask Matthew: "Did you intend to blame all Jews, now and forever, for Jesus' death?" When encountering the end of the parable of the vineyard, which states that the owner "will come and destroy the tenants and give the vineyard to others" (Mark 12:9), I ask Mark, "Did you believe that the Jews should be destroyed?" After Jesus' sermon in the synagogue in Nazareth (Luke 4:18–30), implying that those excluded from community are now favored, I ask Luke, "Do you believe that the Gentiles have replaced the people Israel in God's eyes?" The evangelists are evasive in their answers, but I like to think that they would understand the questions.

But why do I ask these questions of the Gospel writers and not of the figures—the Jews, in the case of Matthew, and Jesus, in the other two examples—to whom the evangelists attributed these words? The answer lies in the relationship between the Gospels and the life and times of the people who appear in them. The Gospel writers did not merely record received tradition, but they also adapted this material to the needs of their congregations. Jesus spoke to a predominantly Jewish audience, the people of Galilee and Judea in the 20s and early 30s of the first century C.E. These peasants, artisans, merchants, tax collectors, and Pharisees lived under direct (in Judea) or indirect (in Galilee) Roman domination; the governor of Judea, Pontius Pilate, is known from several historical sources for his cruelty, greed, and disrespect for the people he ruled. The Gospels themselves were written decades later. Mark is usually dated around the year 70, the time of the destruction of Jerusalem's Temple in the first Jewish revolt against Rome; Matthew and Luke are generally accorded dates ranging from ca. 85 C.E. to the early second century.

Not only time but also setting creates a distance between Jesus and the evangelists. The New Testament is not written in Aramaic, the vernacular in Judea and Galilee, but in *koinē*, "common" Greek. As accounts passed from the disciples of Jesus to the disciples' own followers, from Jerusalem to Damascus, Antioch, Egypt, and Rome, from Jews to Gentiles, and from Aramaic to Greek (and to the numerous translations of today), changes inevitably occurred. What Jesus intended is not necessarily the message the evangelist received, and what the evangelists intended is not necessarily what people in the local congregation, let alone Christians for the past two millennia, heard.

Change occurred not only in the process of transmission but also in response to changing circumstances and ideas. Each evangelist adapted the message for new congregations and in light of developing concepts of who Jesus was and what his death signified. Mark, for example, remarks that Jesus "declared all foods clean" (7:19). In antiquity as well as today, many Jews adhered to the dietary practices proclaimed in Scripture, such as the avoidance of blood products, pork, and shellfish. But it is highly unlikely that Jesus himself ever proclaimed all foods to be fit for consumption. Had Jesus himself settled the kashruth question, Acts and the Pauline letters, written twenty to seventy years after his death, need never have struggled with the question of whether Gentile converts needed to keep the dietary laws.

Luke's Gospel makes it clear that already, by the last part of the first century, its author knew of "many" varying, or competing, accounts of Jesus' life. "Since many have undertaken to set down an orderly account of the events that have been fulfilled among us, just as they were handed on to us by . . . eyewitnesses and servants of the word," Luke writes, "I too decided, after investigating everything carefully from the very first, to write an orderly account" (1:1–3). But how "accurate" Luke was is unclear. Missing from this Gospel are stories well known from the Gospels of Mark and Matthew, such as the feeding of the four thousand, the healing of the Syro-Phoenician/Canaanite woman's daughter, and the visit of the magi. Nor does Luke have Jesus deliver a "Sermon on the Mount." Luke's prologue also returns us to the question of the author's intent. Did Luke write to replace the other Gospels, to correct them, to supplement them? Did Luke even have copies of the other Gospels, and, if so, were they the same as the ones we have in the New Testament today?

The first three Gospels are called "Synoptic," from the Greek for "see together"; their stories are similar to one another in both plot and content. These similarities, however, do not mask important differences. These differences reflect the various materials inherited by the evangelists, their own experiences and literary artistry, and their perceptions of the needs of their respective communities. The Gospels are not objective reports, but proclamations of faith.

Although church tradition knows the Gospels as the work of specific individuals, none of the earliest manuscripts of the Gospels bears its author's name. Irenaeus, a church father writing in Gaul at the end of the second century, was the first to refer to the Gospel writers by the names Matthew, Mark, Luke, and John. Of the Synoptics, Matthew's Gospel is the only one ascribed to a follower of Jesus; Matthew 9:9 mentions one "Matthew sitting at the tax booth" (Mark 2:13–17 and Luke 5:27–32 identify this tax collector as "Levi"). Luke's Gospel is so called because it is associated with "Luke, the beloved physician" (see Col. 4:14; 2 Tim. 4:11; Phlm. 24); Acts (also written by the same author) depicts the narrator as Paul's traveling companion. These texts may well preserve some eyewitness evidence, but even so, their relation to historical reality is complicated. As we all know, memory bears a complex relationship to "what really happened." In retelling a story, details may drop away, elements may be added or omitted, and the story line may change.

While oral tradition certainly played an important role in shaping the Gospel accounts, the Synoptics also have a literary relationship with one another. A majority of biblical scholars hold that the Gospel of Mark appeared first and that Matthew and Luke, independently of each other, used Mark's text as a source. Over 90 percent of Mark appears in Matthew, and approximately 50 percent appears in Luke. Beyond this, Matthew and Luke also share material absent from Mark (e.g., the Beatitudes, the "Lord's Prayer"). For this reason, scholars propose that these authors, again independently of each other, had access to another source, now lost, commonly known as "Q" (from the German *Quelle*, "source"). A minority view proposes that Matthew was the first Gospel, that Luke used Matthew as well as additional information gained from "eyewitnesses and servants" and others (Luke 1:1–4), and that Mark conflated the texts of Matthew and Luke while editing them for brevity. All three Gospels drew on another source held in common: the Greek translation of the Jewish Scriptures, known as the Septuagint.

Our view of the literary relationships among the Gospels will deeply affect our interpretation of each individual Gospel. If we suppose that Matthew changed a Markan text, we then can consider why Matthew made certain changes to Mark, and from this we can deduce some of Matthew's own concerns and interests. Similarly, if we argue that Mark adapted the Gospels of Matthew and Luke, then we will assume that we have easier access to Mark's own agenda. Given the present deadlock on "solving" the so-called "Synoptic problem"—that is, the questions surrounding the relationships among these Gospels—I will note source-critical issues only when they are particularly relevant to the subject of anti-Judaism.

Also elusive is the exact setting of each document. Unlike Paul's letters, which at least note the audience—"to the Thessalonians" or "to the Romans"—the Gospels provide no specific details about audience or setting. We must look for clues within the texts themselves. For example, Mark explains Jewish customs such as the washing of hands prior to eating (7:1–15). He also offers translations of the Aramaic terms: *Talitha cum* ("Little girl, get up" 5:41); *Ephphatha* ("Be opened," 7:34); and Jesus' cry, *Eloi, Eloi, lema sabachtani?* ("My God, my God, why have you forsaken me?" 15:34). From these points we surmise that Mark's audience includes people from outside Aramaic-speaking areas. A location in Rome or Alexandria thus becomes more likely than one in Syria or Galilee. Mark also notes that "the Pharisees, and all the Jews, do not eat unless they thoroughly wash their hands, thus observing the tradition of the elders, and when they come from the market place, they do not eat unless they purify [or 'baptize'] themselves; and there are also many other traditions that they observe, the washing of cups, pots, and bronze kettles [some manuscripts add 'beds']" (Mark 7:3–4 mg.). These comments suggest an author unfamiliar with Judaism, since not all the Jews engaged in such practices. Matthew lacks these explanations (15:1–20); Luke omits the story entirely.

Perhaps our greatest challenge is to determine the author's agenda. Does the text support the community's theology and practice, correct them, or offer new models? Even if we could unequivocally discern an author's intent, we still cannot know how each text was originally received, and whether or how it affected people's beliefs and behaviors. For example, according to Mark (10:11–12) and Luke (16:18), Jesus unilaterally forbade remarriage after divorce; according to Matthew (5:31–32), Jesus permitted divorce only in the case of an illicit sexual act (Greek: *porneia*). Theories abound to explain the injunction and to argue about which version of the teaching, Mark's or Matthew's, is closer to that of Jesus himself. Meanwhile, countless numbers of divorced and remarried people consider themselves biblically faithful, and find no contradiction between their personal circumstances and their Christian beliefs.

Such obstacles complicate the task of determining whether and to what extent the Synoptic Gospels and Acts are anti-Jewish. Nevertheless, we can say much about the ways in which anti-Jewish readings of the Gospels and Acts arise, and we can also assess whether and how both historical and literary investigation can address these interpretations. Our procedure is threefold: first, to describe the setting and issues of the evangelists; second, to focus on specific passages that contribute to anti-Jewish impressions; third, to suggest where careful scholarship can propose alternatives to the teaching of contempt.

MARK

Mark may seem somewhat removed from direct confrontation with Judaism. We have already noted that he describes Jewish practice incorrectly in Mark 7. Further, Mark uses the term "Jew" or "Jews" (*Ioudaios, Ioudaioi*) only five times, each time in the designation "King of the Jews" (15:2, 9, 12, 18, 26), each spoken by a Gentile, and each in the context of Jesus' crucifixion. Mark clearly believes that Jesus *is* the King of the Jews, but this belief does not constitute an anti-Jewish sentiment per se.

Mark's subject matter, of course, requires the presence in his narrative of various Jewish individuals, such as the disciples and those whom Jesus heals, as well as several different groups, such as the Pharisees, Sadducees, Herodians, chief priests, and elders. Most of his individual Jewish characters fare rather well. Only Herodias is clearly evil; her husband, Herod Antipas, is described as "deeply grieved" about having to order John the Baptist's execution at his wife's behest (Mark 6:17–29). The disciples are depicted as normal, that is, flawed, human beings. They frequently misunderstand Jesus' teachings (e.g., 8:14–21); one of them betrays Jesus (14:10, 43–45), three fail him in Gethsemane (14:32–42); one denies him three times (14:66–72), and all forsake him and flee (14:50). Still, Mark's Jesus largely tolerates their failings and expects their reconciliation (16:6–7). Many Jews outside the circle of disciples appreciate Jesus: they marvel at his teachings and seek his healing powers. Jesus cures numerous Jews who express faith in him, including a man with an unclean spirit (1:23–27), a leper (1:40–44), a paralytic (2:1–5), a man with a withered hand (3:1–5), and blind Bartimaeus (10:46–52). A Jewish woman anoints Jesus for burial (14:3–9), and Joseph of Arimathea, "a respected member of the council" (15:42–46), entombs his body. Even Jairus, "one of the leaders of the synagogue" (5:22), expresses faith in Jesus' healing abilities, and Jesus performs a miracle in response to his plea (5:35–43). Thus, while the Markan Jesus advises his followers to take heed, because "you will be beaten in synagogues," the story of Jairus hints at possible reconciliation between Jesus and synagogue leaders (13:9; see also Matt. 10:17–22).

Mark is far more critical of Jewish groups than he is of most Jewish individuals. Historically, Pharisees, Sadducees, and the other groups differed from one another and even among themselves in terms of theology, religious practice, and relationship to the Romans, but Mark depicts them all as united in opposition to Jesus. The Gospel thereby exposes areas of conflict between those who confess Jesus to be the Messiah and those who do not. These conflicts include disputes about Jesus' status as the son of David and as the Messiah (12:35–37), and about Jesus' or his followers' failure to observe certain traditions (7:1–23). Controversy also rages around Jesus' ability to grant forgiveness of sin. In Mark 2:6–7 some scribes ask: "Why does this fellow speak this way? It is blasphemy! Who can forgive sins but God alone?" In the context of first-century Judaism, these questions fall well within the range of acceptable dispute. Jesus himself was certainly a figure who provoked both praise and condemnation, criticism and controversy, in his own time. Mark's accounts of such conflicts, however, may also reflect disputes that his own community had with Judaism.

In the Gospel accounts, the controversy between Jesus and these Jewish groups reaches its climax in the Passion narrative. For Mark, a number of Jewish groups are instrumental in Jesus' arrest and execution. Earlier, in Galilee, the Pharisees plot with the Herodians "to destroy" Jesus (Mark 3:6; see also 10:2 and 12:13). Once Jesus arrives in Jerusalem, the scribes, chief priests, elders, and members of the Sanhedrin plot his death (11:18, 27; 14:1, 43, 53; 15:1, 31). Whether and to what degree this account is anti-Jewish depends in part on our reading of the Jewish crowd's role in the tragedy. If we view them as complicit with the leaders' agenda, then Mark's Gospel has substantial anti-Jewish potential, particularly because the crowds may stand in for the Jews in Mark's own time. If the crowds are seen as innocent, or as manipulated by the leaders, the anti-Jewish implications of the text are reduced.

Similarly ambiguous are three other elements in Mark's narrative that have most often been regarded as anti-Jewish: the so-called "messianic secret," the "cleansing" of the Temple (11:15–19; Matt. 21:12–13; Luke 19:45–48; John 2:13–17) and the parable of the Vineyard (12:1–12; see also Matt. 21:33–46; Luke 20:9–19). I hope to show that all these elements can also be read in ways that do not support anti-Judaism.

The "Messianic Secret"

This is scholars' designation for Mark's portrayal of Jesus as being secretive about his true identity. According to Mark, Jesus commands that people report neither his miracles nor his messianic identity. For example, Jesus sternly warns the leper whom he cures in Mark 1:40–42 to "say nothing to anyone" (1:44). Why does Mark present Jesus in this way? If this theme goes back to the historical Jesus himself, we may speculate that he may have feared that the Romans, or more likely their client ruler in Galilee, Herod Antipas, might order Jesus executed as he did John the Baptist. If the theme is Markan, as is likely, we may suggest a more theological motive: to stress that Jesus' crucifixion, and not his power to work miracles, was the most important marker of his messianic identity. In one notable case, however, Mark's Jesus urges someone not to keep this silence, but to break it. In 5:1–20, Jesus exorcises a "legion" of evil spirits from the "Gerasene demoniac." He then, unusually, commands the healed man to announce to his friends "how much the Lord has done for you" (5:19). Some scholars suggest that Mark is here showing that the "good news" belongs not to Jews, but to the Gentiles, as the name "Legion" (a Roman military unit), the "great herd of swine," and the erstwhile demoniac's mission in the Decapolis (a group of Hellenistic cities most of which are east of the Jordan and the sea of Galilee). If so, then the story itself conveys the anti-Jewish message that the Jews are no longer worthy of God's salvific attention. But two points complicate this reading. First, Jesus generally ordered a cured individual to reenter his or her own community. Thus, just as Jesus exhorts the Jewish leper in 1:44 to go to the priest in order to be officially integrated into society, so the (probably) Gentile demoniac is told to visit his own people, that is, the Gentiles. Second, because there was also a substantial Jewish presence in the Decapolis, nothing in Mark's text suggests a restricted mission. Thus careful attention to literary details of the story and its historical background can guard against an anti-Jewish reading of the "messianic secret" motif.

The "Cleansing of the Temple"

This account describes how Jesus "began to drive out those who were selling and those who were buying in the Temple, and he overturned the tables of the money changers and the seats of those who sold doves, saying, 'Is it not written, "My house shall be called a house of prayer for all the nations?" [Isa. 56:7] But you have made it a den of robbers.'" (Mark 11:15–19). Hollywood treatments only exacerbate the popular image Christians have of the Temple as an institution that banned women and Gentiles, oppressed the people with purity laws, burdened them with taxes, and restricted access to God. According to this view, the Temple was peopled by greedy merchants and money changers, the latter sometimes confused with money lenders, who cheated the populace. None of this is factual, and here too history can help correct anti-Jewish views.

First, nothing in the text speaks of greed or fiscal exploitation. A "den" is not where people are robbed, but rather a hideout where the robbers feel safe. The condemnation thus concerns complicity, not criminality. Further, money changers were needed to convert numerous local coinages into the one standard unit accepted by the Temple. (Today, most Americans do not put lira, marks, or yen into the collection plate; if they did, someone would have to exchange it—"money-change" it—so that the church could put it to use.) The merchants also served an essential function: to supply sacrificial animals. Pilgrims from Europe, Asia Minor, and Africa did not bring their offerings with them, lest the animal become damaged and so unfit for sacrifice. Monies paid to the Temple not only funded its upkeep and paid for community rituals (as do the dues that members pay to their religious institutions today), they also were used for social welfare such as almsgiving. Second, despite the impression left by the citation of Isaiah 56:7, the Temple Jesus entered was already a house of prayer for all nations. Their presence was specifically welcomed in the largest area within the Temple compound, called "the Court of the Gentiles." Jewish women, too, had their own court. Mark 12:41–44 even depicts a woman making an offering in the Temple: "A poor widow came and put in two small copper coins, which are worth a penny." It is, finally, inappropriate to argue that the tearing of the Temple curtain (15:38; the tradition is unique to Christian sources) opens access to God for everyone. Temple architecture itself, as well as much Jewish thinking of the time (especially the concept of the "righteous Gentile") indicates that everyone had this access. Not all Jews believed one had to be Jewish in order to be in a right relationship with heaven.

Similarly, allusions to the Temple's destruction may support an anti-Jewish theology. An anti-Jewish reading of the text would argue that the account of the withered fig tree that frames the "cleansing" (11:12–14, 20–21) anticipates its destruction, Jesus' statements in 13:1–2 confirm it, and Mark's report of the tearing of the veil symbolizes it. To such a reader, the likelihood that the evangelist wrote in approximately 70 C.E., immediately after the destruction of the Temple, suggests one explanation for the debacle: the Temple and those who held it dear (that is, the Jews) rejected Jesus, and so God destroyed their Temple. This argument, however, is theologically untenable. Not only does it open the possibility that any disaster can be interpreted as a sign of divine displeasure, it also too easily locates the divine on the side of the oppressor, rather than on the side of the victim. It is no more theologically appropriate to claim that the destruction of the Temple represents divine rejection of the Jews than it is to claim that the conquering of Christian Jerusalem by the Muslims in the seventh century represents the divine rejection of the church.

The Parable of the Vineyard

Like other parables, this is deceptively simple. The parable genre, known also from Jewish sources, uses images from daily life to provoke listeners to see the world in a new way. We readers struggle with such open-ended stories; we prefer to be told what something means rather than to work out our

own tentative answers. The parables have been subjected to numerous interpretations, many of which have anti-Jewish implications. Mark 12:1-12 (like
the parallels in Luke and Matthew), tells of a man who plants a vineyard,
leases it to tenants, and leaves the country. The tenants slay the slaves sent by
the owner to collect his share of the produce. The owner finally sends his son,
but the tenants kill him also. The parable promises that the owner will
destroy the tenants and give the vineyard to others. It is often argued that the
vineyard represents Israel (Isa. 5:1–7 facilitates the allegory), the tenants are
the Jews, the murdered heir is Jesus, and the owner is God. The others who
will be given the vineyard are the Gentiles, definitely breaking the covenant
between God and Israel. In light of the destruction of the Temple, this reading is compelling.

   This conclusion, however, is flawed. First, in both Jesus' time and the time
of the Gospels, Rome was already the ruling power in Judea. Thus, the "others" of the parable need not be Rome or a Gentile group, and the import of
the parable need not be political. In Jesus' own context, ca. 30 C.E., the parable may have signaled a change in Jewish authority, with Jesus and his followers representing the new (Jewish) leadership. This replacement of the
priestly tenants with Jesus' group is supported by Mark's gloss: "The stone
that the builders rejected has become the cornerstone" (12:10). Second, the
parable's audience within the Gospel itself is not "the Jews" as a whole but
rather the "chief priests, the scribes, and the elders"—all of whom Mark associates both with the Temple and with Jesus' execution. Finally, Mark does not
distinguish between Jews and Gentiles on the basis of virtue. The Gospel
depicts faithful Jews, as we have seen, as well as faithful Gentiles, such as the
Syrophoenician woman (7:24–30), and the centurion at the cross who proclaims Jesus a "God's son" (15:39). Just as there are evil Jews, so there are evil
Gentiles, from Pilate himself to the "whole cohort" who mocked and struck
Jesus before they crucified him (15:16–20). These soldiers were doing more
than just following orders. To identify the tenants as the Jews and the new
owners as the Gentiles imposes on Mark's parable an ethnic distinction
unsupported by the rest of the narrative and creates an anti-Jewish reading
where one need not be found.

   Mark's community was likely dominated by Gentile members who saw the
Gentile world as central to the future of their movement. But this does not
mean that they read Mark's Gospel in an anti-Jewish manner, nor does it mean
that we must do so. Instead, this text may be read as a criticism of fellow Christians who do not recognize the centrality of Jesus' suffering, who insist on
being leaders rather than followers (10:35–45), and who fail to show complete
loyalty to Mark's Jesus, and so to Mark's community as well.

MATTHEW

Matthew's narrative is often considered the "most Jewish" of the Gospels. The five teaching discourses that structure the Gospel—Sermon on the Mount (chaps. 5–7); missionary instructions (10:1–24), parables (13:1–52); church governance (chap. 18); and eschatology (chaps. 24–25)—recall for some readers the Torah, or the "five books of Moses." Matthew in particular preserves the traditions of Israel. His Gospel anchors Jesus' actions to Jewish Scripture by using the "fulfillment formula" ("this was done to fulfill what was spoken by . . . ," 2:23 and frequently elsewhere) to link them to specific biblical passages. Furthermore, Matthew does not depict Jesus as breaking with Jewish law and tradition. In contrast to Mark, Matthew does not state that Jesus "declared all foods clean" (Mark 7:19). Instead, the Matthean Jesus insists that he has "come not to abolish [the Law (Torah) and the Prophets] but to fulfill" (5:17), for "not one letter, not one stroke of a letter, will pass from the law until all is accomplished" (5:18). Matthew's Jesus not only accepts the commandments; he also intensifies them. For example, in the Sermon on the Mount, Jesus expands the prohibition against murder to prohibit anger as well (5:21–26), and extends the injunction against adultery to forbid lust also (5:27–30). The Gospel even has Jesus assert that "the scribes and the Pharisees sit on Moses' seat; therefore do whatever they teach you and follow it" (23:2).

The label "most Jewish" is, of course, relative. Compared to Mark, Matthew presents more that is amenable to traditional Jewish teachings; compared to the Mishnah (the early-third-century C.E. codification of Jewish law), the text is hardly "Jewish." Again we find a problem with labels. Just as there is no consensus on what constitutes "anti-Judaism," so too it can be difficult to determine what is "Jewish." We see this problem even today: Are "Jews for Jesus" Jews (as they consider themselves), or are they "Christians" (as many in both church and synagogue would argue)? If a Jew converts to Roman Catholicism or United Methodism, is she still "Jewish"? If so, in what sense, and who has the authority to bestow the label?

Perhaps the identification of the author helps us to determine whether or not his Gospel is anti-Jewish. Two factors argue against such a facile conclusion. First, we cannot conclusively determine the author's background or the audience's composition. Israel's Scriptures, so prominent in this text, were, by the late first century C.E., also the Scriptures of the Gentile church. The Gospel itself suggests that part of Matthew's original audience was comprised of Gentiles (e.g., 28:19). Thus the Gospel's frequent quotation of the Jewish Scriptures does not necessarily mean that the author or audience considered themselves to be Jewish. Second, and more important, even if it could be definitively determined that Matthew's group was a Jewish splinter sect, the effect of the Gospel's language on relations between "Matthean" and "non-Matthean" Jews would still be negative. Those who remained in the "non-Matthean" synagogue would certainly see its rhetoric as aimed at them, and at all other Jews who did not accept Jesus as the messiah.

Matthew's community, perhaps located in Galilee but more likely in Syrian Antioch (the early-second-century bishop, Ignatius of Antioch, cites the Gospel) and likely dated sometime after 70 C.E., defined itself over and against the synagogue. Although today, in the West, Jews are in the minority and Christians in the majority, the opposite situation prevailed in the first-century Mediterranean: Matthew's church—Matthew is the only Gospel to use the term "church" (*ekklesia*, 16:18; 18:17)—was the smaller group. For Matthew, the "Jews" (*Ioudaioi*) are those who deny the resurrection and believe that the disciples stole Jesus' corpse (28: 13–15).

Matthew's usage of *Ioudaioi* does not mean that the Gentiles displace or replace the Jews as the people of God. Rather, the Gospel insists that through Jesus, membership in the one people of God has been extended to the Gentiles. Both Jews and Gentiles are, for Matthew, targets of evangelism. Nevertheless, those Jews who resist the "good news," especially their leaders, face the most truculent of Matthew's reproaches. Three examples—the infancy narratives, the cure of the centurion, and the Great Commission—will demonstrate the illegitimacy of applying a replacement theology based on ethnic identity to Matthew.

The Infancy Narratives

Some readers find the beginnings of replacement theology in Matthew 1 and 2. Matthew offers a positive depiction of the Gentile magi and a negative one of the Jewish "Herod . . . and all Jerusalem" (2:3). But the narrative does not depict a Jewish/Gentile split, as it is sometimes argued. The "Holy Family" (Jesus, Mary, Joseph) is also Jewish. Jesus' genealogy (1:1–17) securely locates him in the family of Abraham and David. Joseph's dreams assure him that what appears to be a humiliating situation—Mary's premarital pregnancy—is instead the sign of God's plan. This Joseph evokes that earlier dreamer, Jacob's son Joseph, once sold into Egyptian slavery but later able to rescue the family of Israel. Matthew's emphasis is not Jew vs. Gentile, but rather the powerful vs. the powerless; Jerusalem (the capital city) vs. Bethlehem ("by no means least," 2:6) and outlying areas; the static and complacent center vs. the mobile, faithful periphery.

The Gentile Centurion

These observations hold for Jesus' encounter with the centurion, into which interpreters have also read the replacement theme. After his encounter with the Gentile centurion seeking a cure for his paralyzed servant, Jesus announces, "Truly I tell you, in no one in Israel have I found such faith. I tell you, many will come from east and west and will eat with Abraham and Isaac and Jacob in the kingdom of heaven, while the heirs of the kingdom will be thrown into the outer darkness, where there will be weeping and gnashing of teeth" (8:10–12). These "heirs" are often interpreted as the Jews, and "the many from east and west" as the Gentiles. Yet the verse defines neither the "many" nor the "heirs." For Jesus' own audience, and possibly for Matthew's as well, the "many" would be associated not with Gentiles, but with Diaspora Jews. This inclusion is consistent with the Jewish view that the messianic age will witness the ingathering of the people Israel. Moreover, Jesus applies the label "children of the kingdom" to his own disciples in Matthew 13:38, where the saying addresses neither ethnicity nor religiosity, but power. Given that the Matthean Jesus entrusts his disciples, and especially Peter, with the "keys of the kingdom" (16:19), we should not read 8:10–12 as a rejection of ethnic Judaism. Finally, the stories surrounding the centurion's request all feature faithful Jews: a leper (8:2–4), Peter's mother-in-law (8:14–15), a paralytic and his friends (9:2–8), Matthew and his fellow tax collectors (9:9–10), a hemorrhaging woman and a local leader (9:18 –2b), two blind men (9:27–31), and a mute demoniac (9:32–33).

The Great Commission

Jesus' command to "make disciples of all the Gentiles" (*ethnē*, also translated "nations") is often seen as confirming the end of the Jewish mission: the Jews have rejected Jesus, so they are rejected as the mission turns to the Gentiles. Yet Matthew nowhere abrogates the Jewish mission proclaimed by Jesus. Matthew's Jesus instructs his disciples to "Go nowhere among the Gentiles, and enter no town of the Samaritans, but go rather to the lost sheep of the house of Israel" (10:5b–6; 15:24). The Great Commission does not end the Jewish mission, it inaugurates the Gentile one as a second step in salvation history.

The Gospel focuses neither on ethnicity nor even on confession, but on appropriate leadership and use of power. Matthew's Gospel does identify Jesus as the source of salvation (1:21–23; 10:32–33; 26:28, and elsewhere), but it also proclaims that the final judgment is based on one's deeds, not on one's theology. The Sermon on the Mount focuses not on Jesus, but on God and on the proper understanding of Torah. Love of God and love of neighbor (the "Great Commandment") are the hallmarks of Jesus' message (22:37–39), along with the practice of mercy (9:13; 12:7). These commandments come directly from Jewish teaching (Deut. 6:5; Lev. 19:18; Hos. 6:6). Matthew 25 depicts a final judgment in which the separation of (good) sheep from (bad) goats is based on charitable action and love of neighbor, not baptism or belief.

The concern for appropriate action applies also to Matthew's contrasting Jerusalem, which "kills the prophets and stones those who are sent to it," (23:37), as well as towns such as Capernaum, Chorazin, and Bethsaida (11:20–24), with open places of refuge and celebration, such as the desert of John the Baptist, the mountains where sermons are given and thousands are fed. The Gospel praises those who are willing to leave domestic comforts for the sake of Jesus and the kingdom: the peripatetic magi; the faithful Joseph, who takes mother and child from Bethlehem to Egypt and then to Galilee; the men and women who follow Jesus from Galilee to Jerusalem. It praises those who seek Jesus' healing power: the Canaanite woman who demands an exorcism for her demon-possessed daughter (15:21–28); the Jewish woman who snatches a healing from Jesus by touching him secretively (9:20–22). To divide the Gospel into "good Gentiles" and "bad Jews" is to misread it.

Matthew directs its most sustained invective against the abuse of power. In chapter 23, Matthew's Jesus condemns the Pharisees seven times: "Woe to you, scribes and Pharisees." Here Jesus accuses these leaders of hypocrisy and also labels them "brood of vipers," murderers, and "child[ren] of hell." One common argument seeks to exculpate Matthew of the charge of anti-Judaism by comparing this chapter with the rhetoric of Israel's prophets. That is, Jesus' charges against the Pharisees are seen as no different from, and no worse than, the biblical prophets' charges against Israel's leaders. This argument holds when we imagine Jesus himself as addressing these words to other Jews, as the prophets addressed their criticisms to members of their communities. But once these words are placed in the context of Matthew's Gospel, this argument no longer applies. Matthew's Jesus is not the historical Jesus. The Gospel is not addressed to a synagogue, nor is it preserved by the Jewish community. By embedding Jesus' words, if Jesus indeed ever uttered them, in his Gospel, Matthew breaks the rhetorical connection between Matthew 23 and the Israelite prophets. Jesus' words are no longer addressed to fellow Jews but to a different group altogether, a group that includes Gentiles, a group whose story consists not only of their founder's bitter condemnation of these Jewish leaders but also of these leaders' banding together to kill him.

Because Matthew 23 also condemns those who follow the "scribes and Pharisees," it may express a more inclusive anti-Jewish agenda. As Jesus puts it: "Woe to you, scribes and Pharisees, hypocrites! For you cross sea and land to make a single convert, and you make the new convert twice as much a child of hell as yourselves" (Matt. 23:15). For this Gospel, the followers of the Pharisees, those who remain in the synagogue, are children of hell.

Some scholars have argued that such polemic is merely conventional Jewish discourse, no different from the rhetoric used by the authors of the Dead Sea Scrolls or the first-century historian Josephus. This comparison deflects the problem of New Testament anti-Judaism. First, the Dead Sea Scrolls were not promulgated among Gentiles, nor are they implicated in the massacres of any group. Even if Matthew's polemic is conventional, its effect ultimately is to create enmity between church and synagogue. Second, to compare one document with a corpus of hundreds of texts skews the data. If we were to take all Christian texts from the first three centuries—writings against heretics, or against Jews, or against pagans—and compare this corpus to the literary remains from the Qumran caves, the Christian texts would emerge as equally if not more hate-filled. Third, this argument has the effect of blaming Judaism for the New Testament's polemic. In modern parlance, this is known as "blaming the victim." Jews hardly had a monopoly on polemical commentary. Finally, the Gospel, unlike the Dead Sea Scrolls, claims that the "enemies" (however configured) *killed* the leader of their movement.

The verse that has caused more Jewish suffering than any other in the Christian Testament is the uniquely Matthean cry attributed to "the people as a whole": "His [Jesus'] blood be on us and on our children!" (27:25) This verse is often read as implying that all Jews, of Jesus' time and forever afterward, accept the responsibility and blame for Jesus' death. Christian Europe witnessed centuries of pogroms promulgated by church members, inflamed by sermons about the Jews' "blood guilt," who rushed to Jewish homes (often in ghettos established by Christian governments) to avenge their Lord. While the violence has mostly subsided, the charge remains. I have been accused of being a "Christ-killer"; so have my children.

Critical investigation offers another interpretation of Matthew 27:25. First, the scene is unlikely to have any historical basis. We have no evidence that Pilate released prisoners in Judea as a boon to the local population. To the contrary, Jewish and Roman sources both attest to Pilate's complete insensitivity to the Jewish population he governed. Similarly, it strains credulity to believe that Pilate would offer the crowd not only a murderer but also an insurrectionist (Mark 15:7; Matt. 27:16 calls him a "notorious prisoner"). Nor does the timing of this scene make sense. If Barabbas is released to celebrate the Passover feast, he is released a day late: all three Synoptics (unlike John's Gospel) insist that the Last Supper—held the previous evening—is the Passover meal. Finally, several early manuscripts indicate that Barabbas had a first name, "Jesus" (27:16). Thus he serves the purpose not of history, but of theology: Jesus the "Son of the Father," the innocent, dies so that "Jesus, the son of a father" (*bar* is "son" and *abba* "father" in Aramaic), the guilty, can be set free.

Concerning the blood cry itself, "the people as a whole" did not shout for Jesus' death: among the "Jews" are such faithful followers as the women from Galilee and Joseph of Arimathea. In turn, these geographic designations provide one hint concerning the meaning of the verse. Matthew 27:25 is neither historical recollection nor a condemnation of all Jews. Rather, it is a very specific reflection by the evangelist on the fate of Jerusalem. From the narrator's note that "Herod . . . and all Jerusalem" (2:3) were disturbed at the news of the Messiah's birth to Jesus' condemnation of the city as "kill(ing) the prophets and ston(ing) those who are sent" to it (23:37), Matthew's Gospel displays animosity to the capital. Indeed, Matthew is the only Gospel to depict a resurrection appearance not in Jerusalem, but in Galilee (Mark anticipates but does not recount it). The depiction intimates more than the evangelist's aversion to the center of power: it also reflects historical reality. In 69–70 C.E. the Romans starved the population of Jerusalem by cutting off food supplies; in 70 the Temple was destroyed. Matthew, like other followers of Jesus, regarded Jerusalem's destruction as just punishment for its rejection of Jesus. By speaking of the blood on Jerusalem's children, the Gospel reflects a specific past; it does not predict, let alone enjoin, a global future. Today the verse is sometimes taken as a hopeful wish that Jews will accept the blood of Jesus. Unfortunately, this less violent interpretation may be just as pernicious. If all Jews proclaim the atoning death of Jesus the Messiah, the verse will have the same anti-Jewish effect: there would be only the *ekklēsia*; there would be no more "Judaism."

LUKE

Although the Third Gospel and its companion piece, the Acts of the Apostles, are traditionally assigned to Luke, the companion of Paul, the identity of the author and the social context of these works remain debated. Some have argued that Luke is Jewish, given especially the presentation of Jewish piety manifested by Elizabeth, Zechariah, Mary, Joseph, and Jesus in Luke 1–2, the continual focus on Jerusalem, and Acts' insistence that the church is in full continuity with the teachings and traditions of Israel. Alternatively, some have suggested that Luke has Gentile emphases, including Simeon's prediction that the child will be "a light for revelation to the Gentiles" (2:32) and Acts' description of the extension of the church "to the ends of the earth" (1:8). Some scholars adopt an intermediate position by suggesting Luke is a God-fearer, that is, a Gentile affiliated with a synagogue, who honored the teachings of the Torah and perhaps voluntarily practiced many of the mitzvoth (commandments), but who did not formally convert to Judaism.

This lack of consensus also characterizes scholars' assessments of Luke's view of Jews and Judaism. It may even be that the narrative itself is inconsistent. In combining stories from a variety of sources, the evangelist may well have juxtaposed generally pro-Jewish material with more negative accounts. Moreover, even where Luke depicts Jews and Jewish tradition positively, the point of this presentation seems to be less to praise Judaism than to *coopt* its position as the covenant community. It is clear that Luke, like Mark and Matthew, sees the future of the community of believers as residing among the Gentiles: this Gentile community, then, is the heir of Israel's traditions.

Although the initial chapters in Acts recount the affiliation of thousands of Jews in Jerusalem with the new movement, the apostles, the Hellenists (likely Greek-speaking Jews in Jerusalem who accepted Jesus as the Messiah), Paul, and his companions are invariably persecuted by "Jews." Paul himself is introduced as an arch-persecutor who consents to the martyrdom of Stephen and attempts to initiate persecutions of believers in Jerusalem and Damascus. Once he himself becomes a believer and apostle, Paul consistently begins his mission in synagogues, is repeatedly rejected by the vast majority of Jews, and three times insists that only the Gentiles will receive the message of salvation. In Acts 13:46, he as well as Barnabas proclaim to "the Jews" that "Since you reject it [the word of God] and judge yourselves to be unworthy of eternal life, we are now turning to the Gentiles." Acts 18:6, reminiscent of Matthew 27:25, is more vituperative: "Your blood be on your own heads! I am innocent. From now on I will go to the Gentiles." Finally, in Acts 28:26, after citing Isaiah 6:9–10—"You will indeed listen, but never understand, and you will indeed look, but never perceive" (cf. Matt. 13:14–15; John 12:40)—Paul once more announces that "this salvation of God has been sent to the Gentiles; they will listen."

A closer look at Luke 4 (Jesus' sermon in, and subsequent expulsion from, the Nazareth synagogue) further illustrates Luke's ambivalence. This passage is traditionally seen as depicting irrational Jewish hatred of Jesus and as anticipating the violence that "the Jews/the synagogue" will do to his followers. Closer reading requires us to modify this view. At first, the Jewish population entirely supports Jesus' proclamation of the "the year of the Lord's favor" (4:19; following Isa. 61). The promises associated with the messianic age, such as liberation from captivity, would be especially welcome for a population chafing under Roman domination. But then Jesus denies the promises to his own people by stating that God's goodwill did not go to Jews, but to Gentiles such as Naaman the Syrian whom Elisha healed, and the widow of Zarephath fed by Elijah. The people in the synagogue are then described as dragging

Jesus to a cliff with the intention of throwing him off. It is not clear who rejects whom first. Thus, for Luke, local Jews who worship in synagogues are not friends of God or the church. For Luke's readers, the synagogue is immediately established as a place of irrational hatred, of danger, and of rejection of its own Scripture.

Some scholars conclude that Luke's continuing emphasis on Gentiles, coupled with the Gospel's various unique stories of women (e.g., the focus in the infancy accounts on Mary and Elizabeth, and the bent-over woman in the synagogue in 13:10–17), points to Jesus' mission to the disenfranchised and the outcast. This conclusion implies that *Judaism* has disenfranchised or cast out women and Gentiles. We have already seen that Judaism welcomed women and Gentiles into the Temple. Luke 13:10-17 shows women in synagogues (that bent-over women is neither on a balcony nor behind a curtain). There is no reason to believe that Gentiles are disenfranchised or outcast. I sincerely doubt that Pilate or the various centurions depicted in the Gospels and Acts saw themselves as outcasts. Not only were Gentiles the majority group in the Empire, they were welcomed by Jews as both God-fearers and as proselytes, both in synagogues abroad and in the Temple in the capitol.

Like the other Synoptic Gospels, Luke's text is replete with faithful Jews. But the same scenes of opposition, especially from the leadership, appear as well. Scribes, Pharisees, and synagogue leaders challenge Jesus' authority (5:30–32; 6:1–5, 6–11; 11:53–54; 13:14–17; 14:1–6; 15:2; 16:14). Even in cases where a Pharisee initially welcomes Jesus, the scene deteriorates into a critique of the Pharisee's behavior (e.g., 7:36–50; 11:37–44). A verse unique to Luke places the blame for the cross squarely on the "scribes and chief priests" who "watched [Jesus] and sent spies who pretended to be honest, in order to trap him by what he said, so as to hand him over to the jurisdiction and authority of the governor" (20:19–20). Hypocrisy combines with jealousy and vindictiveness. If Luke's audience associates all contemporary Jews with these Jewish leaders, anti-Jewish readings are the likely result.

It is sometimes argued that Luke distinguishes between "good" and "bad" Pharisees. In Luke 13:31, certain Pharisees warn Jesus that Herod is plotting to kill him. In Acts, Gamaliel, "a Pharisee in the council . . . respected by all the people" (5:34) advises the "fellow of Israelites" (5:35) to release Peter and John lest by hindering them from preaching, they also hinder the word of God. Nevertheless, neither the Pharisees in the Gospel nor Gamaliel himself joins the Christian movement, and so by implication, in Luke's narrative, they do not understand their own Scriptures. Moreover, Luke notes that Gamaliel was Paul's teacher (Acts 22:3). Since Paul's pre-Christian identity is marked by his persecution of the church, we can only wonder what it was that he learned at Gamaliel's feet.

By describing Paul's involvement with "persecution" of those Jews who were confessing Jesus in the Diaspora, Luke creates the impression that Jews were violent and irrational in their response to Jesus. History offers an alternative view. Rather than posit some sort of witch-hunt, it is more likely that some Jews found Jewish Christians to be both disruptive and dangerous. Most benignly, it is unlikely synagogue members would have found Christian Jews' praising of Jesus to be congenial. (I suspect the same negative reaction would occur were a follower of the Reverend Moon to interrupt a local Presbyterian or Methodist service.) Nor would they have appreciated any insistence that anyone not adhering to the gospel message was bound for hell. Equally reprehensible would be any Christian denunciation of Jewish leaders and practice. In the face of pressure from a Gentile world that knew about the Jewish (and Samaritan) revolt against Roman rule in Judea and Galilee, Christian claims of a new king who stood in the place of Caesar would also be problematic. From annoyingly disruptive to politically dangerous, Christians within the Jewish fold would have appeared to their nonmessianic families and friends as needing serious instruction in Judaism 101.

We should also be less sanguine about assuming that each example of Christian polemic is a reaction to synagogue persecution. Just as Shakespeare portrayed his vengeful Shylock at a time when Jews had no significant presence in England, so it is possible that Luke's portrayal of Judaism is not a reflection of his community's direct experience of Jews. Anti-Jewish rhetoric does not require Jews.

It may be helpful to consider how some of the material Luke presents might have sounded, not to Christian ears in the late first or early second century, but to Jewish ears at the end of the Second Temple period. Among the parables unique to Luke, the parable of the Prodigal Son (15:11–32) and the parable of the Pharisee and the Tax Collector (18:9–14) are often interpreted in an anti-Jewish manner. Yet in neither case is this the only, or indeed the best, interpretation.

The Prodigal Son

The younger son is typically viewed as the Christian who was once lost to sin, but then repented and was received back by the gracious father. The older son, hearing the noise of the feast (had no one thought to invite him?), protests to his father: "For all these years I have been working like a slave for you, and I have never disobeyed your command; yet you have never given me even a young goat so that I might celebrate with my friends" (Luke 15:29). For many commentators, the elder son represents the Pharisees or all Jews, as people whose slavery to the law was joyless, judgmental, and filled with resentment.

As we saw with interpretations of the Vineyard parable, allegorical readings are to an extent arbitrary. There is no compelling reason to equate the younger son with Christians or the older son with Jews. Indeed, there is no compelling reason to see the parable as an allegory. Not all fathers, rich men (16:19–31), or judges (see 18:1–8) must represent God. Not all those "found" represent the redeemed sinner. The lost sheep and the lost coin, whose accounts are linked with that of the lost son, surely do not "repent." Further, we might note what the father does tell his older child: "Son, you are always with me, and all that is mine is yours" (15:31). The verse should prevent any supersessionist interpretation. To the contrary, it raises a very personal question: How will the elder treat the younger, once the father is gone?

The Parable of the Pharisee and the Tax Collector

This is often used to contrast Pharisaic (i.e., Jewish) hypocrisy with Christian piety. Luke provides an explanation for the parable by depicting Jesus announcing at its end, "I tell you, [the tax collector] went down to his home justified rather than the [Pharisee]; for all who exalt themselves will be humbled, but all who humble themselves will be exalted" (18:14). It may have been the case, however, that on Jesus' own lips the interpretation of the parable was much more subtle, and much more profound. On the one hand, the reader is set up to dislike the pompous, self-righteous Pharisee, who gives thanks that he is "not like other people." How many faithful, however, then or now, actually take the time to give thanks that we have not succumbed to the ever-present temptation of being "thieves, rogues, adulterers"(18:11)? The Pharisee contrasts himself with the tax collector, but so too would most of Jesus' original audience. Tax collectors were in the employ of the Romans; to many, they represented traitors who made a living by bleeding the people, and, after siphoning off their own cut, contributed to the upkeep of the Roman occupation. Thus the original reader is caught: to judge the Pharisee harshly creates sympathy for the otherwise hated tax collector.

More disturbing yet, the tax collector, although praying, "God, be merciful to me, a sinner!" (18:13), returns to his house still a tax collector. He asks for mercy, but he does not reform his life. For Luke, who will present several righteous tax collectors (including Levi [5:27–32] and Zaccheus [19:1–10]), the tax collector is a good man who is too often judged unfairly. Both matters are not so simple. Once readers decide they would much rather identify with the tax collector than with that self-righteous Pharisee, they do exactly what the parable warns against: they judge others, proclaim themselves better than others, and perhaps even seek cheap grace (it is the Pharisee, not the tax collector, who gives tithes and fasts twice a week). Again, locating statements and sayings in terms of Jesus' original audience, rather than interpreting them only through the eyes of the Christian evangelists, provides a historically grounded means of mitigating anti-Jewish interpretations.

For Luke, finally, the Jews as a whole are responsible for the death of Jesus. The speeches in Acts make the point explicit: "Let the entire house of Israel know with certainty that God has made him both Lord and Messiah, this Jesus *whom you crucified*" (Acts 2:36); "But you rejected the Holy and Righteous One and asked to have a murderer given to you, and *you killed the Author of life*" (Acts 3:14–15); "Jesus Christ of Nazareth, *whom you crucified*" (Acts 4:10); "Which of the prophets did your ancestors not persecute? They killed those who fore-told the coming of the Righteous One, and now *you have become his betrayers and murderers*" (Acts 7:52, emphases mine). This litany of charges shows that anti-Jewish readings are not always imposed on the text, but rather, they can be present in the text itself. For the author of Acts, "the Jews" continue to per-secute the apostles and Paul, the synagogue remains a place of danger and rejection, and the future of the church is among the Gentiles.

A CAUTIONARY CONCLUSION

Scholars, particularly those influenced by postmodernism, sometimes argue that a text has no intrinsic meaning, and that meaning is imposed on a text by the reader. Certainly, readers bring their own concerns to the process of find-ing meaning. But I cannot endorse this argument as the best solution to the problem of anti-Jewish interpretations of the Gospels and Acts. Texts are not innocent, nor are they open to any interpretation the reader wishes to pro-pose. To regard Hitler's *Mein Kampf* as not being intrinsically anti-Jewish, or the proclamations of the KKK as not of themselves racist would be, at the very least, naive. Granted, this comparison is extreme. The Gospels and Acts do not commend to their audiences the killing of Jews or forcing them into ghet-tos. The Synoptic authors would, I believe, be appalled at what has been done to Jewish communities in Jesus' name for close to two millennia. Neverthe-less, these texts do plant seeds that, with certain types of fertilizer, yield an anti-Jewish growth.

This investigation into the details of the Synoptic Gospels and Acts, the likely historical settings of the material received by the evangelists, and the evangelists' own social contexts, reveals both how easy it has been for the anti-Jewish readings to develop as well as how those readings, by appeal to these same texts, can be countered. At times, literary-critical observation disrupts a stark division between Jew and Gentile; at times, historical observation sus-pends anti-Jewish assumptions. Nevertheless, neither historical nor literary nor any other critical method can resolve the question of whether the Synoptic Gospels and Acts were written with an anti-Jewish agenda and/or whether they were read as anti-Jewish by their original audiences. At best, we can, and should, seek to expose anti-Jewish traditional readings as well as those passages that lend themselves to such readings. Studying these texts in mixed Jewish and Christian settings often brings the damaging passages to the fore. The material should not be glossed over or simply proclaimed problem-free. As any Jew who has ever experienced what he or she would call "anti-Judaism" can attest, the problem has not gone away. We can and should provide some explication for what the material is doing in a text that is held by the church to be inspired Scripture. We can and should recognize that a text need not be interpreted anti-Jewishly, and, at the same time, we can and should acknowledge that such interpretations sometimes have solid historical grounding.

The conclusions historians draw remain at best highly educated conjectures. Moreover, even if we could firmly conclude that the evangelists and their audiences did not have anti-Jewish views, the fact remains that throughout the subsequent centuries, later Christians have often interpreted the texts in this manner. Divorced from any historical context, many of the passages in the Gospels and Acts remain a challenge for those who would seek to improve Jewish-Christian relations.

There is much in the New Testament that the vast majority of contemporary Christians no longer take literally, from the insistence in 1 Timothy 2 that women gain their salvation by bearing children, to the claim in Revelation that the only ones to be saved are 144,000 male virgins from the twelve tribes of Israel (Rev. 14:1–4). Through history, through what some would call the actions of the Holy Spirit, texts that negate the fullness of human life, texts that appear to enjoin evil, slavery, or war, are given new interpretations. The time is surely here for the anti-Jewish texts, or, perhaps put better, the texts that can be and have been seen as anti-Jewish, to undergo the same critical, merciful treatment.

5

The Gospel of John: How "the Jews" Became Part of the Plot

Adele Reinhartz

The Gospel of John has long been known as the "spiritual Gospel." Its portrait of Jesus as the Divine Word is both uplifting and challenging. Its description of Jesus as "the way, and the truth, and the life" (14:6) and of believers as "born" of water and the Spirit (3:5–7) are familiar to Christians and non-Christians alike. Yet this spiritual Gospel contains some harsh and decidedly unspiritual statements. Most notorious is John 8:44. In this verse, Jesus declares to a group of Jews: "You are from your father the devil." This association of the Jews and the devil has had a long and tragic afterlife in Western art, literature, and theology. But the Gospel is not entirely negative about Jews and Judaism. In fact, the Gospel of John is intimately tied to the Judaism of its time. The Gospel portrays Jesus as a Jew whose life revolves around the Jewish festivals, and whose identity as the Messiah is confirmed by the Jewish Scriptures. Any attempt to understand this Gospel, to live by it, or to appreciate its legacy must therefore address not only its profound theology but also its complex representation of Jews and Judaism.

Before turning to this issue, a few introductory remarks are in order. The Gospel of John is also known as the "Fourth Gospel," due to its placement after the Gospels of Matthew, Mark, and Luke in the New Testament. The Fourth Gospel was written in Greek, in the late first century C.E., perhaps in a city in Asia Minor (modern-day Turkey), such as Ephesus. It went through a lengthy period of composition before reaching its present form. This process may have included historical reminiscences, early traditions, and the use of an earlier written source that told of Jesus' "signs" or miracles. The identity of the individual(s) who set their stamp on the Gospel is unknown. The narrative itself points to the anonymous "beloved disciple," who enjoys a favored position with Jesus, as the authority whose witness is preserved in the Gospel (e.g., 21:24). The traditional identification of this disciple with John, the son of Zebedee, is not generally accepted by New Testament scholars.

In its present form, the Gospel begins with a poetic prologue describing Jesus' existence with God before the creation of the world (John 1:1–18) and concludes with an epilogue describing how the risen Jesus commissions Peter as the new shepherd of his flock (John 21). One passage—the story of the adulterous woman—that appears in most printed editions of the Fourth Gospel (7:53–8:11) was probably not part of the original Gospel, since it is absent from some ancient manuscripts and appears elsewhere in other manuscripts.

John 20:30–31 describes the primary purpose of the Gospel in these terms: "Now Jesus did many other signs in the presence of his disciples, which are not written in this book. But these are written so that you may come to believe [or continue to believe] that Jesus is the Messiah, the Son of God, and that through believing you may have life in his name." Although the Gospel may have been directed at least in part to those who were not *yet* believers, the overall tone and content suggest that it was written within a particular community of believers in order to strengthen their faith in Jesus and to deepen their understanding of his significance in their individual and communal lives.

In keeping with this purpose, the Fourth Gospel focuses extensively on Christology, that is, on the exploration of Jesus' identity as the Messiah and Son of God. Christology underlies all other elements of the Gospel, including its plot, its characterization, and its theology. The Gospel depicts Jesus as traveling from Galilee to Jerusalem and back for a period of over two years. Throughout, Jesus performs "signs" that reveal his identity as the Messiah and Son of God to those who are able and willing to understand them. The characters illustrate the various responses to Jesus, including Mary and Martha's profound faith (John 11), the Samaritan woman's hesitant but growing faith (John 4), Nicodemus's incomprehension (John 3), and the Jewish authorities' refusal to believe (John 12). This Gospel's complex theology, including its eschatology (understanding of the end times) and soteriology (understanding of salvation), all derive from its Christology. As the Son of God, Jesus comes from God and mediates the relationship between God and humankind. Jesus is "the good shepherd" (10:11), the "light of the world" (8:12), and the source of eternal life (6:40). No knowledge or experience of God is possible except through him (14:6). The exclusiveness of this claim contributes considerably to the Gospel's attitude toward those Jews who refuse to believe in Jesus.

THE GOSPEL'S NARRATIVE LEVELS

In sorting out the various elements of the Gospel's treatment of Jews and Judaism, it is useful to distinguish among the various narrative levels or stories that are intertwined in the Gospel as a whole. Each of these stories has its own setting, its own characters, and its own plot dominated by conflict between the hero and his opponents.

The primary narrative level is the story that is apparent on the "surface" of the Gospel. This story tells what we might call a "historical tale," in the sense that it situates Jesus within a specific historical setting. The scenes that make up the narrative take place in Judea, Galilee, and Samaria, during the prefecture of Pontius Pilate, Rome's representative in Judea, some decades prior to the Jewish revolt against Rome of 66–70 C.E. The hero is Jesus, a Galilean preacher, healer, and miracle worker. His opponents are the Jews and their authorities, who believe that this man, who his followers claim is the long-awaited Messiah and king of Israel, poses a threat to their community in light of its delicate relations with Rome (11:50).

The second narrative level is more subtle, though its contours are apparent in the Gospel's prologue in 1:1–18 and in Jesus' many lengthy discourses. This level tells a "cosmological tale" that provides the broader chronological, geographical, and theological framework for the historical tale. This level has the cosmos as its setting and eternity as its time frame. Its hero is the preexistent Word who becomes flesh and comes into the world to bring salvation. Its villain is the "ruler of this world" (14:30), "the evil one" (17:15), Satan (13:27), or the devil (8:44; 13:2). Its plot describes the origin of the hero in the divine realm, his descent into the world, his mission to humankind, his defeat of the "ruler of this world," and his return to the Father.

Dimly perceptible in the shadows of these two tales is yet a third story, that of the "Johannine community." This narrative level may be called the "ecclesiological tale," from the Greek word *ekklēsia*, meaning assembly, gathering, or church. The Fourth Gospel nowhere uses the word *ekklēsia*; neither does it prophesy the founding of a community, as does Matthew 16:18, or spell out the rules and principles that should govern such a community, as do the letters of Paul. Nevertheless, the very nature of this Gospel, with its distinctive story line and theology, implies the existence of a community within which and for which the Gospel would have been written. Between the lines we may discern some of the problems in this community as it struggled to establish and define itself within the Greco-Roman world.

These three narrative levels or tales intersect at many points. For example, Jesus' crucifixion marks the outcome of the Jewish authorities' plot against

Jesus within the historical tale; it is also the moment of Jesus' ascension and return to the Father within the cosmological tale; and it signals the coming of the Paraclete, that is, the Spirit of truth, who will guide the Johannine community in its ongoing effort to understand Jesus as the Christ and Son of God. As we shall see, Jewish characters and Judaism as a religious system play important and varied roles within each of these three tales. Each level represents and treats Jews and Judaism in ways both positive and negative.

JEWS AND JUDAISM IN THE HISTORICAL TALE

The Fourth Gospel has an overall Jewish "feel." It takes for granted some of the divisions and groupings in the Jewish ethnic, religious, and political landscape to which other texts, most notably the works of the first-century Jewish historian Josephus, also refer. The references to the Pharisees, as well as to the group around John the Baptist, imply the existence of diverse communities within Jewish society at that time. Also acknowledged are the tensions between Samaritans and Jews. After Jesus asks the Samaritan woman for a drink in 4:7, she comments, "How is it that you, a Jew, ask a drink of me, a woman of Samaria?" The narrator then draws attention to the fact that "Jews do not share things in common with Samaritans" (4:9). Implicit throughout is the context of Roman domination, particularly in Judea but perhaps also in Galilee (cf. 4:46–54, in which an official, usually considered to be a Roman, asks Jesus to heal his son). The presence of Roman power affected all Jews, leaders and rank and file, including the fledgling group emerging around Jesus.

Jesus and most of the other characters in the Gospel are Jews, and they participate fully in the Jewish world of early first-century Palestine. They live according to the Jewish calendar, Sabbath, and festivals (e.g., 2:13; 5:9), and they congregate within Jewish institutions such as the Temple and the synagogue (6:59; 7:14). They discuss matters of Jewish law and relate their own experiences to events in Jewish Scripture (5:39; 6:32). They apparently engage in Jewish customs such as ritual handwashing before meals (2:6), and giving thanks for bread before eating a meal (6:11). They follow Jewish burial practices such as anointing the body and covering it with a shroud (19:40).

Jesus' christological identity is in large measure expressed in Jewish terms. The prologue describes him as God's Wisdom, in a manner that draws explicitly from the Jewish Wisdom tradition (see Prov. 8, Sir. 24). The disciples recognize him as the Messiah prophesied by Scripture (John 1:45) and proclaim him the "King of Israel" (1:49). Thus the Johannine concept of the individual who fulfills this messianic ideal, as well as the concept of salvation itself, are deeply rooted in Judaism. In this sense, salvation originates "from the Jews," as John's Jesus declares to the Samaritan woman (4:22).

The Jewish identities of Jesus and his followers are taken for granted. Yet despite their obvious Jewishness, the label "Jew" is applied to Jesus only once (by the Samaritan woman, 4:9), and to his followers and disciples never. There are even passages in which the Johannine Jesus explicitly dissociates himself from Judaism. Jesus sets himself outside and above Jewish law. In 8:17 and 10:34, he refers to Jewish law as "your law"; in 5:17 he declares that he is not bound by the Sabbath laws because of his unique relationship to the Father. Furthermore, Jesus' discourses employ such a sharp dichotomy between Jesus and believers on the one hand, and the unbelieving Jews on the other, that the term "Jew" cannot comfortably be used to describe the Jesus we find in this Gospel. Finally, the presentation of Jesus as Messiah attracts those outside the Jewish community despite the fact that many of the messianic titles have Jewish referents. Both the Samaritan woman's recognition of Jesus as the fulfillment of the messianic expectations of her community (4:25, 29), as well as the Greeks' interest in Jesus (12:20–21) make this point.

This effort to distance Jesus from Judaism coheres with the Gospel's portrait of the Jews as those who refuse to believe that Jesus is the Messiah and Son of God. Typical is 5:37-47, according to which Jesus accuses the Jews of not heeding the divine witness to Jesus' identity: "The Father who sent me has himself testified on my behalf. You have never heard his voice or seen his form, and you do not have his word abiding in you, because you do not believe him whom he has sent" (5:37–38).

Even more sinister are the Jews' acts of violence. The Jews persecute Jesus for healing on the Sabbath (5:16), and, more to the point, for calling God his own Father, "thereby making himself equal to God" (5:18). In 8:59 and 10:31 the Jews take up stones to hurl at Jesus. After Jesus raises Lazarus from the dead, Jewish authorities plot Jesus' death in earnest. Shortly thereafter, Jesus is arrested by a detachment of Roman soldiers and by police sent by the chief priests and Pharisees (18:3, 12). He is interrogated by Annas, the father-in-law of Caiaphas the high priest (18:19–23) and by Caiaphas himself (18:24). Only then is he sent to Pontius Pilate (18:28–40). Pilate finds him innocent (18:38) and then offers to release him, but the Jews refuse. Finally, the chief priests and police shout, "Crucify him! Crucify him!" The narrative leaves no doubt that, although Pilate gave the formal order for Jesus' execution, the moral responsibility for Jesus' death lies with the Jewish authorities. The Jews' verbal and physical abuse is directed not only at Jesus but also at those who believe in him. After Jesus heals the lame man by the Pool of Beth-zatha, the Jews chastise the man for carrying his mat on the Sabbath (5:10). The blind man's parents fear that they will be expelled from the synagogue if they describe how their son was healed and by whom (9:22). Persecution and even death awaits the disciples, according to 16:2.

In sum, the Jews play the role of Jesus' opponents in the historical tale. The Jews, or at least their authorities, are directly responsible for Jesus' death on the cross, despite the fact that it is Pilate who gave the final order for Jesus' crucifixion. They oppose his interpretations of the Scripture and his self-understanding as the Messiah and Son of God, and they also physically endanger him and his followers.

JEWS AND JUDAISM IN THE COSMOLOGICAL TALE

The Gospel bases its view of God's relationship with humankind primarily on the Hebrew Bible. For this reason, the Johannine worldview has much in common with that expressed in Jewish writings from the same era. For example, the prologue depicts Jesus as the divine Word who is with God and is instrumental in the creation of the world. This portrait owes much to the wisdom tradition of Proverbs and other texts that feature a female wisdom figure who aids God in the process of creation (Prov. 8:27–31). The God in question is the creator God of Israel; the people to whom Jesus comes are the Jews, who view themselves as God's chosen people.

Within Jewish tradition, the idea of chosenness relates closely to the concept of covenant, that is, the belief that God and Israel enjoy a relationship characterized by mutual love, commitment, and jointly recognized obligations. This intimate covenantal relationship is made concrete in the Torah (the Pentateuch; five books of Moses), which God gave to Moses at Mount Sinai after the exodus and by which Israel strives to live.

The Gospel of John implicitly works with a similar understanding of the relationship between God and his people. God loves the world and is concerned for the salvation of humankind (3:16). The Torah is God's word and hence carries authority (5:39). The Johannine view differs from other Jewish perspectives, however, in the role it assigns to Jesus in the divine covenant. God's love for the world is expressed in the fact that he sent his Son to bring salvation (3:16). As God's Son, Jesus becomes the medium through which humankind now comes to God and comes to know God (14:7). The Torah itself prophesies Jesus' coming and hence bears witness to his identity as Messiah and Son of God (5:46). Jesus and the Jews may argue, in traditional Jewish fashion, over the correct interpretation of the Torah, but they all accept its divine nature and authority.

Marring this harmonious picture is the claim that each side makes to an exclusive relationship with God. Just as Jews believed their covenantal relationship to God to be unique and exclusive, so too did the Fourth Evangelist believe that *his* understanding of Jesus' role as the new mediator of divine love and salvation replaced or precluded all other views. This commitment to exclusivity comes to the fore in the role to which the Fourth Evangelist assigns the Jews within the cosmological tale.

Throughout the Gospel, the evangelist expounds upon the superiority of his vision of salvation through Christ. He does so in large measure through the use of contrasting metaphors. One set of metaphors describes dichotomous states of being, such as light/darkness, life/death, above/below, from God/not from God. The other set comprises dichotomous activities, such as believing/disbelieving, accepting/rejecting, doing good/doing evil, loving/hating. The positive element of each pair is associated with Jesus, the negative element of each pair with those who oppose Jesus and reject the claim that Jesus is the Christ, the Son of God.

These paired terms assert the existence of two types of people. Those who belong to the light, have life, who come from above and from God, also believe, accept, do good, and love God. They believe Jesus to be the Messiah and Son of God and know him to be the path to knowledge of God and salvation. The Gospel challenges and exhorts its readers to be part of this group, that is, to believe in Jesus as Messiah and Son of God, "that through believing you may have life in his name" (20:31) The other group is associated with the negative terms in each pair: darkness, death, from below, not from God. These people do not believe or accept; they do evil and hate God. Thus they are opposed to Jesus in both word and deed.

Although these paired terms often appear in passages that have a general and universal application, the Gospel consistently and directly associates the negative pole with explicitly Jewish characters within the narrative. In 1:4 and 8:12, for example, the Gospel describes Jesus as the light of the world. The light challenges the darkness that has tried but not succeeded in overcoming it (1:4). The light, as Jesus, came into the world in order that believers not remain in darkness (12:46). Some, however, love darkness rather than light because their deeds are evil (3:19). Though "darkness" is an abstract metaphor, it characterizes the Jews both as a group and individually. In 3:2, Nicodemus, a Pharisee and leader of the Jews (3:1), comes to Jesus "by night." In 8:12, Jesus promises the Jews: "Whoever follows me will never walk in darkness but will have the light of life." But the Jews' absolute rejection of Jesus excludes them from this promise (12:37). A consequence as well as a cause of their being in darkness is their inability to see. Their blindness is contrasted with the newfound vision of the man born blind who declares Jesus to be the Son of Man (9:39-41).

A similar move occurs with respect to the range of paired activities associated with each state of being. The most fundamental of these is believing and disbelieving. Belief in Jesus is evidence of faith in God (12:44); the one who sees Jesus also sees God (12:45). The Jews, on the other hand, do not believe and do not see God, because they do not believe in Jesus as the Christ and Son of God (5:38). In 5:43–44, Jesus chides his Jewish listeners: "I have come in my Father's name, and you do not accept me; if another comes in his own name, you will accept him. How can you believe when you accept glory from one another and do not seek the glory that comes from the one who alone is God?" Accepting Jesus demonstrates a love for God, for Jesus, and for fellow believers (15:12–17). Rejecting Jesus is tantamount to hating God. Jesus accuses the Jews of not having the love of God in them (8:42), and tells the disciples that his enemies hate both himself and his Father (15:23–24).

Consistent with this dualistic rhetoric is the claim that the Jews are children not of God but of the devil (8:44). This claim is perhaps a logical inference from the evangelist's conviction that in rejecting Jesus, the Jews distance themselves from God. But if we consider this accusation in its context in John 8, a more complex argument emerges.

John 8:31–59 takes the form of a controversy between Jesus and a group of Jews who had believed in him but apparently no longer do so (8:31). The essence of this controversy concerns precisely the question of their different and mutually exclusive ways of understanding the covenantal relationship. These Jews assert their self-understanding as God's chosen people, linked to God through the Torah, whereas Jesus argues vigorously that God has now redrawn the rules so that relationship with God can be experienced only through Jesus his Son.

This passage is not the transcript of a conversation that took place between the "historical Jesus" and the "historical Jews" of his time. Rather, like the rest of the Gospel, it is entirely "scripted" by the Fourth Evangelist. It is the evangelist, through his narrator, who provides the lines for both Jesus and the Jews. Nevertheless, the controversy over the ways in which humans can and should relate to God rings true insofar as it coheres well with other texts that describe the theological issues at stake between Jews and the believers in Jesus.

Key to the Jews' understanding of themselves in relation to God are three statements: that Abraham is their father (8:33, 39), that they have never served or been enslaved to anyone or anything (8:33), and that they are children of God (8:41). Together these claims express the Jews' commitment to monotheism as the foundational tenet of their faith. This commitment is expressed in biblical passages that are cornerstones of Jewish theology and prayer. The Shema, which became a pivotal element of Jewish liturgy, proclaims: "Hear, O Israel; The LORD our God, the LORD is One" (Deut 6:4, margin). The opening section of the Decalogue declares God's uniqueness and singularity: "I am the Lord your God, who brought you out of the land of Egypt, out of the house of slavery; you shall have no other gods before me. You shall not make for yourself an idol, whether in the form of anything that is in heaven above, or that is on the earth beneath, or that is in the water under the earth. You shall not bow down to them or worship them" (Exod. 20:2–5). Both of these texts assert God's uniqueness and call on Israel to worship God alone.

The Jews' self-identification as children of Abraham recalls Abraham's status as the patriarch of the Jewish people. This status is based entirely on his role as the first monotheist, that is, as the first to recognize the one God as the creator of the world. According to postbiblical Jewish tradition, Abraham's father was not only an idolater but also an idolmaker. Though Abraham was raised to follow in his father's footsteps, he was puzzled by the powerlessness of his father's idols, and as he grew up he came to discern the existence of a supreme divine being who, though unseen, was the creator of the natural world in all its beauty and intricacy. Belief in the one God and the commitment to following his will as set out in the Torah make Israel as a nation the children of God.

The Jews' claim that they have never served or been enslaved to anyone is more ambiguous. Taken in a literal, political sense, this statement is blatantly untrue. Jews had indeed been enslaved, most notably to Pharaoh during the period before the exodus. But here the English translation misses the nuances of the Greek. The verb *douleuō*, which can certainly mean "to be enslaved," has another, well-established meaning, namely, "to serve." In many places in the Septuagint (second-century B.C.E. Greek translation of the Hebrew Bible), this verb specifically refers to worship of God or gods. For example, Psalm 106:36 accuses the Israelites of being ensnared by the idols whom they served. In his letter to the Galatians, Paul uses this verb in a way that implies both worship and slavery. He chastises the Galatians, who are of Gentile background, by asking, "Now, however, that you have come to know God, or rather to be known by God, how can you turn back again to the weak and beggarly elemental spirits? How can you want to be enslaved to them again?" (Gal. 4:9; cf. Jer. 5:19). Against this background, the Jews' claim in 8:33, that they have never "been slaves to" anyone or anything, expresses again their profound commitment to monotheism. They have never served any being other than God; indeed, to serve another "divine" being would be tantamount to slavery.

The Jews' self-description as the children of God echoes the Father-son language that is used to describe the covenantal relationship between God and Israel in a number of biblical texts. In Exodus 4:22–23, for example, God coaches Moses on what to say to the pharaoh as he tries to secure Israel's release: "Then you shall say to Pharaoh, 'Thus says the LORD: Israel is my first-born son. . . . Let my son go that he may worship me.'" This claim competes directly with that of the evangelist, namely, that Jesus is uniquely God's son.

In addition to these three claims, the Jews hurl two accusations at Jesus: that he is a Samaritan and that he has a demon (8:48). Now, the Jews here may simply be engaging in the time-honored practice of name-calling. It is unlikely that they really believe that Jesus is a Samaritan (in fact, they know that he is from Galilee; cf. 7:41), or even that he is possessed by a demon. Rather, both insults effectively accuse Jesus of straying from pure monotheism. The Johannine narrator tells us that the Jews would not share vessels with Samaritans (4:9), thereby implying that Jews did not consider Samaritans to be monotheists. According to the book of Jubilees, a postbiblical Jewish work likely dating from the second century B.C.E., the hand of Mastema, that is, the devil, works in those who worship other gods. Therefore in calling Jesus a Samaritan and claiming that he is possessed by a demon, the Jews are accusing him of violating the belief in the one true God.

In this passage, the Jews describe themselves forcefully as participants in a firm and committed covenantal relationship with God, and raise questions about Jesus' own covenantal status. The Johannine Jesus responds by systematically undermining the Jews' claims to this relationship. For Jesus, the Jews' refusal to accept his claims about himself proves that they cannot be the children of Abraham. Unlike Abraham, who accepted God's messengers (Gen. 18), the Jews try to kill Jesus (John 8:40). Though they claim never to have served anyone or anything, the Jews are in fact still enslaved until or unless they come to believe in him. In 8:34–36, Jesus tells the Jews that "everyone who commits sin is a slave to sin. The slave does not have a permanent place in the household; the son has a place there forever. So if the Son makes you free, you will be free indeed." In this way, Jesus is playing on the dual meaning of the term "to serve," meaning both to "be enslaved" and "to worship." Whereas the Jews assert that they have never worshiped any God but the one true God, Jesus declares that they are enslaved to sin and therefore alienated from God, unless they approach God through faith in Jesus as his Son. Finally, the Jews' lack of faith in Jesus as well as their actions show that they cannot be the children of God: "If God were your Father, you would love me, for I came from God and now I am here. I did not come on my own, but he sent me" (8:42). That is, love of God is expressed solely through love of his Son; the fact that they deny that Jesus is the Son indicates that they do not love God and hence cannot be God's children. It is in this context that the infamous "devil" declaration appears. Having connected disbelief in Jesus with hatred of God, and implying that those who hate God cannot be children of God, Jesus can then declare to the Jews that "You are from your father the devil, and you choose to do your father's desires. He was a murderer from the beginning and does not stand in the truth, because there is no truth in him. When he lies, he speaks according to his own nature, for he is a liar and the father of lies." In his view, the Jews' denial of his messianic identity is a lie; their efforts to persecute him are murder. Both of these count against their claim to be the children of God.

Thus the discussion in John 8 is in effect a dispute over radically different views of the relationship between God and his "children," that is, different versions of the cosmological tale. By describing themselves as the children of Abraham and of God, and as never having been enslaved to anyone or as having worshiped other gods, the Jews are staking their claim to an exclusive and binding relationship with the one true God. From the Jewish perspective, Jesus is setting himself up as a god in his own right when he claims to be the Son of God who shares in God's attributes. For this reason, belief in Jesus is *not* the path to the God of Israel, but away from God to idolatry. No flesh-and-blood person can be equal or similar to God, or share in the attributes that are uniquely and singularly divine. Jesus, in turn, denies that the Jews are children of Abraham and of God. He categorically states and restates the claim that relationship to and love of God can only be expressed through acceptance and love of Jesus as his Son. In the black-and-white world of Johannine rhetoric, if the Jews are not the children of God, then they must be the children of the devil.

In John 8, the Fourth Evangelist claims that the new covenant mediated through Jesus supersedes the covenant established on Mount Sinai with the giving of the Torah. Now that the Word has come into the world, he supersedes all previous ways of relating to God. The Gospel also shows Jesus displacing specific Jewish symbols, institutions, and practices. Frequent comparisons with Moses imply that the benefits that Moses was able to provide for his people during the exodus and their long wandering in the desert are far surpassed by what Jesus can provide now in this new salvific moment. One example is found in Jesus' "bread of life" discourse (6:25–58), which follows his miraculous multiplication of the loaves and fish (6:1–14). The Jews who witnessed and partook in this miracle recall the manna or bread that their ancestors received in the desert: "Our ancestors ate the manna in the wilderness; as it is written, 'He gave them bread from heaven to eat'" (6:31). Jesus reminds them that "it was not Moses who gave you the bread from heaven, but it is my Father who gives you the true bread from heaven" (6:32). But the bread Jesus is offering them—his body—is far superior to the bread that they received in the wilderness. "Your ancestors ate the manna in the wilderness, and they died. This is the bread that comes down from heaven, so that one may eat of it and not die" (6:49–50).

Not only is Jesus the "true bread" but he is also God's true Temple. In John 2, Jesus chases the money changers and merchants out of the Temple at the Passover, and apparently prophesies its impending destruction: "Destroy this temple, and in three days I will raise it up" (2:19). The Jews protest: "This temple has been under construction for forty-six years, and will you raise it up in three days?" (2:20). But, explains the narrator, Jesus was speaking of the temple of his body (2:21). To readers already familiar with the tradition that Jesus was raised from the dead on the third day after his crucifixion, this story clearly looks ahead to the passion and resurrection narratives. It implies that the new temple of God is Jesus. As the Son of God, Jesus is the place where the divine spirit now abides.

That Jesus replaces the Temple as God's special place is expressed explicitly in Jesus' conversation with the Samaritan woman (John 4). In 4:19–20, the Samaritan woman says to Jesus, "Sir, I see that you are a prophet. Our ancestors worshiped on this mountain [Gerizim], but you say that the place where people must worship is in Jerusalem." Jesus replies with a prophecy: "Woman, believe me, the hour is coming when you will worship the Father neither on this mountain nor in Jerusalem . . . when the true worshipers will worship the Father in spirit and truth, for the Father seeks such as these to worship him" (4:21–23). The fulfillment of this prophecy begins within the Gospel narrative itself, at the second Passover recounted in the Gospel, when the crowds stream neither to Mount Gerizim in Samaria nor to Mount Zion in Judea, but to the mountain in Galilee where Jesus is (6:1–4).

JEWS AND JUDAISM IN THE ECCLESIOLOGICAL TALE

The mixed representation of Jews and Judaism in the Gospel of John creates a serious problem for readers for whom the Gospel has canonical and authoritative status. Most contemporary readers are willing to concede Jesus' Jewishness and the ways in which New Testament texts draw on Jewish texts and the geography and culture of first-century Palestine. But the Gospel ascribes a villainous role to the Jews in its historical tale, associates them with the negative terms through the rhetoric of binary opposition in its christological tale, and undermines Jewish covenantal identity in its cosmological tale. In our post-Holocaust era, the problems raised by these elements of the Gospel are particularly difficult. Many theologians, preachers, and committed churchgoers wish to repudiate Christian anti-Semitism, and are sensitive to the varied and often subtle ways in which anti-Semitic stereotypes and sentiments may still persist. Such readers must ask themselves how a text that is so sublime in parts can also say such venomous things about the Jews and still be the Word of God.

The modern academic study of the New Testament often does not address directly such theological dilemmas. Many scholars do, however, attempt to reconcile or, one might even say, to explain away the apparent anti-Jewish rhetoric of both the text and its portrayal of Jesus. One approach is to posit a particular construction of the ecclesiological tale. Unlike the historical and cosmological tales, the ecclesiological tale is not explicitly present in the Gospel narrative, but depends on the prior argument that the Gospel encodes the experience and history of the community. To discern this tale, one must assume that the characters within the Gospel narrative represent the sorts of individuals and groups who may have been part of or known to a historical community of believers toward the end of the first century, and that the events in the Gospel describe experiences that befell that community.

On the basis of these two principles, many scholars argue that the Gospel reflects a profound and traumatic experience of the Johannine community, namely, its expulsion from a larger Jewish community of which it had been a part. This interpretation is based on three passages in the Gospel which state that the Jews expelled "Christ-confessors" from the synagogue. In John 9:22, the parents of the man born blind, whose sight Jesus had restored, are afraid to answer to Pharisaic cross-examination for fear of the Jews, who "had already agreed that anyone who confessed Jesus to be the Messiah would be put out of the synagogue." The notion of expulsion is repeated in 12:42, and in 16:2, which also refers to physical persecution of the disciples at the hands of the Jews. Such expulsion is unlikely to have occurred in the time of Jesus, when his followers were relatively few in number. For this reason, so the argument goes, these passages must refer to the experience of the community in the late first-century, when the Gospel reached its present form. In this construction of the ecclesiological tale, the Jews play a highly negative role in the history and experience of the Johannine community. As those responsible for excluding the Christ-confessors from the synagogue, the Jews contributed directly to the ultimate separation between Judaism and the movement around Jesus.

Although not all scholars accept it, many introductory textbooks, as well as books written for both general and academic audiences, either invoke or presuppose this version of the ecclesiological tale. Its advantages are considerable. In the first place, it supplies a plausible context for the strident debate between Jesus and the Jews throughout the Gospel. Second, by suggesting that the hostile representations of the Jews and statements about them are a response to the act of expulsion, scholars can argue that the Fourth Gospel never intended that its words about "the Jews" be taken as a sweeping condemnation of the Jewish people as a whole, because the Johannine community, in this construction, is itself Jewish. This defuses the fear that the Gospel, a canonical text for Christian churches, may be anti-Jewish.

Ultimately, however, this argument is unconvincing. Viewing the negative representations of the Jews in the historical and cosmological tales as a reasonable response to the Jews' acts of persecution of the community within the ecclesiological tale, or rather, within the historical experience of the community, simply places the responsibility for anti-Judaism on the shoulders of the Jews themselves. This is a seriously flawed line of interpretation, particularly in the absence of evidence that such persecution ever took place.

A second related attempt to resolve the problems posed by the Gospel's representation of Jews and Judaism is to reconsider the meaning and appropriate translation of the term *Ioudaios* itself. How would the first readers of the Gospel, the members of the Johannine community, have understood the Gospel's repeated references to the *Ioudaioi*? Though this issue pertains to the historical and cosmological tales, it ultimately focuses on the ways in which the term would have been understood in the late first century, against the background of the community's experiences in its own social and religious context.

The term *Ioudaios*, often translated as "Jew," as we noted earlier, is almost never used to describe Jesus or his followers. The term appears approximately seventy times in the Fourth Gospel, many more times than in the Synoptics Gospels. In some cases, the usage is neutral and descriptive, as when the narrator refers to Jewish customs (e.g., the Jewish rites of purification, 2:6) or Jewish festivals (the "Passover of the Jews," 2:13). In other cases, the connotation is positive, as when Jesus tells the Samaritan that "salvation is from [or of] the Jews" (4:22). But in most cases the term is used to express a negative view of the Jews as a group, as the ones who reject Jesus, refuse to believe in him, and ultimately plot his death.

Some scholars have argued that the Gospel writer does not use the Greek term *Ioudaios* to refer to someone of the Jewish religion or nationality, as we would have it today, but rather in more specific ways that made sense in the first-century context. Two main alternatives are given. One is the translation of some occurrences of *Ioudaioi* (the plural form) as "Jewish authorities," as distinct from the Jewish people as a whole. Scholars validate this translation by appealing to the text itself, in which it is most often the Jewish authorities who plot Jesus' death or who argue against him. Other scholars suggest that the term emphasizes the geographical rather than ethnic or religious identity of the *Ioudaioi*, who therefore should be considered Judeans rather than Jews per se. This also is plausible, as, for example, throughout John 11, the story of Mary, Martha, and Lazarus, which is set in Bethany, a village in Judea (11:18).

Both of these positions seem attractive in the contemporary discussion of the Fourth Gospel, because both attempt to navigate around the anti-Jewish potential in the rendering of *Ioudaios* as "Jew." If *Ioudaios* is translated as "Jew," there exists the danger that readers may transpose to contemporary Jews the negative role that the *Ioudaioi* play in the Gospel and the negative emotions that they arouse in the reader. Avoiding this translation may thus avoid an anti-Jewish reading of the Gospel.

Nevertheless, to argue that the *Ioudaioi* are not really "the Jews" seems to let the evangelist off a bit too easily, for two reasons. The first is historical. It must be remembered that, according to most scholars, the Gospel itself, while set in Judea, Galilee, and Samaria, was written and circulated in the Diaspora, in which the broader sense of *Ioudaios* as designating a national, religious, political group was already current. Furthermore, the meaning of *Ioudaios*, a complex term from its earliest attestations, changed over time. Before the mid- to late-second century B.C.E., to be sure, *Ioudaios* was primarily an ethnic-geographic term properly translated "Judean." By the second half of the second century B.C.E., however, the term was applied also to people who were not ethnic or geographic Judeans but who affiliated themselves either religiously, by coming to believe in the God of the Judeans, or politically, by joining the Judean state as allies or citizens. By the time the Fourth Gospel was written toward the end of the first century C.E., the term was used to denote both an ethnic-geographic identity and a religious identity that was not limited to Jews who lived in Judea or who were born of Judean parents.

The Gospel's use of the term therefore supports an interpretation of *Ioudaios* that includes ethnic-geographic, political, and religious elements. In places, the term is used in the context of religious customs and beliefs that extend beyond Judea and are characteristic of Jews in the Diaspora as much as in Palestine. For example, the Gospel narrative is punctuated by a number of festivals that are described as feasts of the Jews (2:13, 5:1, 6:4, 7:2, 11:55; cf. also 19:42). The term *Ioudaios* is also used in the narrator's explanations of particular Jewish customs. John 2:6 refers to the water and jars used in Jewish rites of purification, in the context of a wedding that takes place in Cana in Galilee; 19:40 refers to Jewish burial rites that do not seem to be specific to Judea. In the course of Pilate's interrogation, Jesus says that he has spoken openly "in synagogues and in the temple, where all the Jews come together" (18:20). As a political designation, the term is also not limited to Judea. Key here is the sign on the cross that reads "Jesus of Nazareth, King of the *Ioudaioi*." Although the sign may be read in a mocking and sarcastic manner, it nevertheless presumes that it is not implausible for a man from Nazareth, and hence a non-Judean, to claim kingship of the *Ioudaioi*. This suggests that other references to Jesus as king of the Jews may also refer not to Judeans specifically, but to the Jewish nation as a whole. Most explicit is 18:35, in which Pilate declares, "I am not a Jew [*Ioudaios*], am I? Your own nation and the chief priests have handed you over to me." These examples suggest that the Fourth Evangelist is not operating with a narrow and limited definition of *Ioudaios*. While some contexts may permit a narrower translation, the sense in all cases is best met by the direct translation of *Ioudaios* as "Jew," including its connotations of a national but not geographically limited religious, political, and cultural identity.

Most important, the fact that the same word occurs numerous times and in a variety of contexts tends to blur the fine distinctions and nuances implied by these contexts and to generalize the meaning to its broadest possible referent, namely, to the Jews as a nation defined by a set of religious beliefs, cultic and liturgical practices, and a sense of peoplehood. The Gospel does not maintain a rigid distinction between the "Pharisees" or the Jewish leadership and the "Jews." For example, the two labels are used interchangeably in the aftermath of the healing of the man born blind. In 9:13, the "Pharisees" come into contact with the man who had formerly been blind. John 9:18 states that "the Jews did not believe that he had been blind and had received his sight until they called the parents of the man who had received his sight." The interchangeable use of "Pharisees" and "Jews" in these verses, coupled with the fact that the same negative attributes are associated with each of these labels, suggest that the Beloved Disciple is not drawing a careful distinction between the Jews in general and their Pharisaic leadership, or between Diaspora, Galilean, or Judean "Jews." For these reasons, the ecclesiological tale, at least as commonly constructed, may well imply an identification between the *Ioudaioi* who persecuted Jesus and expelled his followers from the synagogue with the *Ioudaioi*—the group and not only its leadership—among whom the Johannine community lived.

Neither of these solutions defuses the anti-Jewish potential of the text. There is in fact no solution that gets the Fourth Gospel "off the hook." It is not possible to explain away the negative presentations of Jews or to deny that the Johannine understanding of Jesus includes the view that he has superseded the Jewish covenant and taken over its major institutions and symbols. Any honest and engaged reading of the Gospel must surely acknowledge, and lament, the presence of these themes.

Such acknowledgment requires that we recognize that the Gospel, while inspired by a particular understanding and experience of Jesus, was nevertheless written by human beings in specific, perhaps very difficult, circumstances. This observation returns us to the ecclesiological tale. It is difficult to demonstrate that the Gospel encodes directly the experience of the Johannine community. The notion that Jews expelled Johannine believers from the synagogue is problematic theologically, because it blames the Jews themselves for the invective to which they are subjected within the Gospel narrative and discourse materials. It is also problematic historically because no external evidence suggests that any Jewish leaders had the authority, the means, or even the incentive to expel Christ-confessors from the synagogue, certainly not in the decade or two after the destruction of the Temple. Nevertheless, we can find some hints within the Gospel of a more complex relationship between Jews and Jewish Christ-confessors than the "expulsion" theory suggests. We can also get a glimpse of the difficult struggle for self-definition within which the Johannine portrayal of Jews and Judaism must be placed.

The Gospel itself contains several stories that may imply a much more positive relationship between the "Christ-confessors" and the Jews among whom they lived. One example is John 11. In this chapter, Mary and Martha of Bethany call on Jesus to come to heal their brother Lazarus, who is deathly ill. Jesus tarries, and Lazarus dies (11: 6, 17). When Jesus arrives in Bethany, he finds Martha and Mary in mourning, surrounded and comforted by many Jews (11:19). Such mourning would be inconceivable in a situation in which the sisters, known publicly as devout followers of Jesus, have already been excluded from the synagogue, that is, from the Jewish community. Another example is 12:10–11, in which the Jewish leaders plot to execute Lazarus as well as Jesus, "since it was on account of him [Lazarus] that many of the Jews were deserting and were believing in Jesus." In this passage, the Jewish leadership is upset about Jews who begin to believe in Jesus; the fact that they equate such belief with desertion implies that they view faith in Christ as incompatible with Judaism. But nothing indicates that the authorities can actually expel Jewish believers in Christ from the Jewish community. The "expulsion" theory cannot accommodate the complex relationships between the Johannine and Jewish communities implied by an ecclesiological reading of the Gospel as a whole.

What purpose is served by the negative representations of Jews and Judaism in this Gospel? Perhaps, given the proximity of Johannine belief to its Jewish roots, the evangelist needed to distinguish his own understanding of salvation and the covenant between humankind and the Divine very sharply from that of other forms of Judaism. This goal could be achieved at least in part by providing a critique of, or at least a diatribe against, Jewish belief apart from Jesus. Perhaps the evangelist intended to persuade his earliest readers that the Jews outside their community intended to persecute them by expulsion or even death. In this way the evangelist might perhaps have hoped to discourage his intended audience from attending synagogue or participating in events in the larger Jewish community.

These observations suggest that the evangelist's portrayal of the Jews may have been shaped not only, or perhaps not even primarily, by the historical experience of the community but by the ideological agenda of the evangelist, by his strong convictions concerning the central christological message that

Jesus is the Christ and the sole way to know God the Father. He argues that by continuing to meet with Jews who are not Christ-confessors, the members of his own community turn their backs on the very faith that they had professed. If so, then it is possible that the Johannine community was not itself expelled from the synagogue, but rather was moving toward formal or institutional separation from the Jewish community. From this perspective, the positive or neutral references to Jews and Judaism point to the close ties between the theology and worldview of the Johannine community and those of Judaism. This itself suggests that many Johannine believers were of Jewish birth and background themselves. The negative representations, on the other hand, reflect the need of this community to define themselves over against other Jews in the context of the painful process of separation.

This perspective allows us to retain some sympathy for the Johannine community without requiring that we rationalize the negative elements in the Gospel's portrayal of the Jews and Judaism. It is unlikely that the evangelist consciously intended his words to reverberate through the centuries, nor, I would hope, would he have condoned the ways in which they have been used to justify anti-Jewish sentiments and actions. Nevertheless, we would be amiss to ignore the strong emotions and hostility that run as an undercurrent through this Gospel, on all of its narrative levels. The Jesus event required not only faith in Jesus as the Messiah and Son of God but also rethinking personal priorities and convictions and forging a community identity and self-understanding with respect to other groups. Such a process is bound to be painful to the extent that it requires the rejection or revision of earlier identities and affiliations. Whereas the ecclesiological tale may be an intellectual exercise undertaken by scholarly readers, the historical and cosmological tales are clearly present within the Gospel itself. They express the evangelist's deep commitment to a particular version of Jesus' life story, and to his own understanding of its profound and world-changing significance for himself and for his community.

Select Bibliography and Suggestions for Further Reading

These suggestions are meant to give some guidance to nonspecialist readers who would like to explore further the topics that organize each chapter. Most of these books will themselves have copious bibliographies and thus further suggestions.

The Origins of Christianity: A useful introduction to Hellenism and Jewish culture is Shaye Cohen's *From the Maccabees to the Mishnah* (Philadelphia: Westminster Press, 1987); see also the collection of essays edited by Steven Fine, *Jews, Christians, and Polytheists in the Ancient Synagogue* (London: Routledge, 1999). On Jesus, Paul, and the ways that earliest Christianity negotiates its movement out of rural Aramaic-speaking Galilee into the wider Greek Mediterranean world, see Paula Fredriksen, *Jesus of Nazareth, King of the Jews* (New York: Knopf, 1999). On the various Christian negotiations with majority culture, see Robin Lane Fox, *Pagans and Christians* (New York: Knopf, 1986), and, with beautiful illustrations, Peter Brown, *The World of Late Antiquity* (New York: Harcourt, Brace, Jovanovich, 1971).

The Historical Jesus: This topic has an enormous bibliography. In addition to the works mentioned in the notes to chapter 2, see especially E. P. Sanders, *Jesus and Judaism* (Philadelphia: Fortress Press, 1985) and *The Historical Figure of Jesus* (London: Penguin Books, 1993). John P. Meier has brought out three volumes of his comprehensive and authoritative consideration of this subject and the scholarship on it in *A Marginal Jew: Rethinking the Historical Jesus* (New York: Doubleday), vol. 1: *The Roots of the Problem and the Person* (1991); vol. 2, *Mentor, Message, and Miracles* (1994); vol. 3, *Companions and Competitors* (2001).

117

Paul: On taking Paul out of the interpretive context of later theology and placing him back in his own historical period and native religion, see K. Stendahl's classic essay, *Paul among Jews and Gentiles* (Philadelphia: Fortress Press, 1976). Three different trajectories from that point of principle are described in: E. P. Sanders, *Paul and Palestinian Judaism* (Philadelphia: Fortress Press, 1976); Lloyd Gaston, *Paul and the Torah* (Vancouver: University of British Columbia Press, 1987); and J. G. Gager, *Reinventing Paul* (New York: Oxford University Press, 2000). For a consideration of Paul as a skilled ancient writer and teacher as well as a committed Jewish apostle to Gentiles, see Stanley Stowers, *A Rereading of Romans: Justice, Jews, and Gentiles* (New Haven, Conn.: Yale University Press, 1994).

The Synoptic Gospels and Acts: The essays in William Farmer's collection *Anti-Judaism and the Gospels* (Harrisburg, Pa.: Trinity Press International, 1999) offer a good introduction to the topic as a whole. For recent studies of the relationship between Matthew's community and Judaism, see Anthony Saldarini, *Matthew's Jewish-Christian Community* (Chicago: University of Chicago Press, 1994) and Donald Senior, *What Are They Saying about Matthew?* rev. and enl. ed. (New York: Paulist Press, 1996). More technical is Dale C. Allison Jr., *The New Moses: A Matthean Typology* (Minneapolis: Fortress Press, 1993). There has been comparably little written on Mark and Judaism; for a very good introduction to Mark that seriously addresses this subject, see Joel Marcus, *Mark 1–8* (Anchor Bible Commentary, New York: Doubleday, 2000). and *Mark 9–16* (Anchor Bible Commentary, New York: Doubleday, forthcoming). For Luke and Acts, see Joseph B. Tyson, *Luke, Judaism, and the Scholars: Critical Approaches to Luke-Acts* (Columbia: University of South Carolina Press, 1999). For treatments of particular passages in Luke and Acts, see Tyson's *Images of Judaism in Luke-Acts* (Columbia: University of South Carolina Press, 1992).

The Gospel of John: For a comprehensive look at the varying approaches to the issue of anti-Judaism in the Fourth Gospel, see R. Bieringer et al., editors, *Anti-Judaism and the Fourth Gospel* (Louisville, Ky.: Westminister John Knox Press, 2001), an anthology of essays by major scholars in the field. J. Louis Martyn's *History and Theology in the Fourth Gospel*, 2d ed. (Nashville: Abingdon Press, 1979) remains the most important exposition of the "expulsion theory," which understands the Gospel's anti-Judaism as the community's response to being expelled from the synagogue. For a detailed consideration of the Gospel's consequences for Jewish-Christian dialogue, see Adele Reinhartz, *Befriending the Beloved Disciple: A Jewish Reading of the Gospel of John* (New York: Continuum, 2001).

Contributors

Paula Fredriksen is the William Goodwin Aurelio Professor of the Appreciation of Scripture at Boston University. Among her publications are *From Jesus to Christ: The Origins of the New Testament Images of Jesus*, 2d ed. (New Haven: Yale University Press, 2000) and *Jesus of Nazareth, King of the Jews: A Jewish Life and the Emergence of Christianity* (New York: Knopf, 1999).

John G. Gager is the William H. Danforth Professor of Religion at Princeton University. He has authored a number of books on ancient Mediterranean religions, among them *The Origins of Anti-Semitism* (New York: Oxford University Press, 1983) and, most recently, *Reinventing Paul* (New York: Oxford University Press, 2000).

Amy-Jill Levine is the E. Rhodes and Leona B. Carpenter Professor of New Testament Studies in the Vanderbilt University Divinity School and the Graduate Department of Religion. Author and editor of many studies on formative Judaism and Christian origins, she has also published *The Social and Ethnic Dimensions of Matthean Salvation History* (Lewiston, NY: Edwin Mellen Press, 1988).

Adele Reinhartz is Dean of Graduate Studies and Research, Wilfrid Laurier University, Waterloo, Ontario. She is the author of many studies of biblical literature, particularly of the Fourth Gospel, including *The Word in the World: The Cosmological Tale in the Fourth Gospel* (Atlanta: Society of Bbiblical Literature, 1992) and, most recently, *Befriending the Beloved Disciple: A Jewish Reading of the Gospel of John* (New York: Continuum, 2001).

E. P. Sanders is Professor of Arts and Sciences of Religion at Duke University. Among his many studies of early Judaism and Christian origins are *Paul and Palestinian Judaism* (Philadelphia: Fortress Press, 1977), *Jesus and Judaism* (Philadelphia: Fortress Press, 1985), *Judaism: Practice and Belief, 63 B.C.E. to 70 C.E.* (Philadelphia: Trinity Press International, 1992), and *The Historical Figure of Jesus* (London: Penguin Books, 1993).

Index of
Ancient Sources

Subject Index